Nils Jönsson-Rose

Window and Parlor Gardening

A Guide for the Selection, Propagation and Care of House-Plants

Nils Jönsson-Rose

Window and Parlor Gardening
A Guide for the Selection, Propagation and Care of House-Plants

ISBN/EAN: 9783337080884

Printed in Europe, USA, Canada, Australia, Japan

Cover: Foto ©Andreas Hilbeck / pixelio.de

More available books at **www.hansebooks.com**

WINDOW AND PARLOR GARDENING

A·GUIDE·FOR·THE
SELECTION, PROPAGATION
AND·CARE·OF·HOUSE-
PLANTS

BY

N. JÖNSSON-ROSE····WITH
ILLUSTRATIONS·BY·THE·AUTHOR

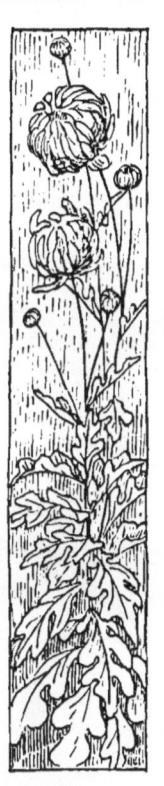

CHARLES SCRIBNER'S SONS
NEW YORK · MDCCCXCV

To those whose cheerful presence brightens a
million homes, to the kind and enlightened
American women, this work is respectfully
dedicated by

The Author.

CONTENTS

PART I

PROPAGATION AND CARE OF HOUSE PLANTS

PART II

THE SELECTION OF HOUSE PLANTS

ILLUSTRATIONS

INTRODUCTION

HE practice of growing plants in windows and apartments is one of the most rational and instructive amusements that can be had.

Unfortunately this simple art is not very assiduously cultivated in this country. Few women here take the same interest in plants as do their sisters of the Old World, and those who do have as yet had no opportunity of gaining a sufficient knowledge of the subject for lack of works of instruction.

Still there is hardly a home in the whole country where plants are absolute strangers, for most people make attempts, at one time or another, to cultivate plants in their windows. That so many discouraging failures are made is not owing to climatic conditions or other natural causes, but chiefly to a bad selection of plants and a want of knowledge as to their proper treatment. Still the culture of most plants is quite simple. Give them sufficient nutriment, water, light, and heat, and they will grow and develop without much other attention.

That which so greatly tends to make a home pleasant and cheerful is, therefore, within the reach of all. There is not a laborer's wife so poor that she cannot have her windows full of flowers, if she has learned or will learn how to take proper interest in such things. There is not a home so humble that it cannot be made noble and refined by the use of plants that can be grown at pleasure for next to nothing.

In Europe this fact has been acknowledged for years, ever since the Linnæan era opened a new world of wonders and of beauty to everybody. Now millions grow plants in parlors and windows ; the countess in her palace tends hers, often with her own hands ; the peasant wife takes no less interest in her more humble flowers. This branch of horticulture has become a necessity, and is especially beneficial in thickly populated cities. To introduce a bit of nature into the house itself is not a mere fad, but it is and will continue to be an important factor of culture and refinement.

Botanical gardens, public parks, and large horticultural establishments have done much to make flowers and plants popular ; but in so peculiar a branch of horticulture as window-gardening, popular guides accessible to everybody are an absolute necessity. In all countries except America numerous books have been written on the subject : some treating exclusively of plants, with brief descriptions and briefer cultural notes ; others going into the details of every operation connected with window-gardening. Of necessity, any descriptive list of plants had to contain quite a number of species, for the reason that some plants were grown in one part of a country, others in other parts ; the rich cherished the more costly ones, and the poor chose varieties easy of culture and rich in flowers. Clearly, all plants enumerated in a work of this kind cannot be grown together in one apartment or one house ; some plants love pure, cool air, and are especially suited to mountain regions and the extreme north ; others enjoy heat and moisture, and may be cultivated anywhere.

Thus it happens that climatic conditions have been the

greatest barriers to the progress of American window-gardening. Plants coming from high altitudes, from snow-covered mountains in the tropics, such as the Fuchsia and the Calceolaria, suffered too much through the excessive heat of summer ; but it was just such plants introduced from Europe that were first tried in this country. Little by little, as horticulture began to advance, it was found that many plants considered tender and tropical in Europe, and for that reason unavailable for home-culture there, were best suited to the American climate. The plants grown for home decoration in most of the States are of a different type from those grown in Europe. Except in mountain regions and in the Northern States, the culture of many Old World favorites becomes tedious and unsatisfactory. But the substitutes are not to be despised.

Palms here take the place of less noble plants. Gorgeous flowers of tropical origin replace the more modest plants of cooler regions. In this respect, therefore, America has the advantage over most parts of Europe. But the American house offers fewer opportunities for growing plants than most houses in Europe. There, especially when French windows are used, the window-sill is very broad and gives room for quite a number of plants. The advantage of having the window opening outward like a door is also apparent. Still, these drawbacks may be easily overcome. The window-sill may be broadened, brackets can be provided for holding plants of many kinds, and a number of plants may be grown with the greatest of ease in any light room, on flower-stands of artistic design. The American house offers, however, many advantages unknown in Europe. When heated by means of steam or hot air, the temperature can be kept more uniform throughout the year. The climate is sufficiently warm, even for tropical plants, for at least six or seven months of the year, and an occasional low degree of heat above the freezing point does not injure any plants, provided the mean annual temperature is sufficient. In well-built stone or brick houses the windows are generally deep and convenient for plant culture. They also offer better facilities for placing window-boxes outside in summer, a method universally used in England, and forming one of the prettiest features of all English towns and villages, where in some parts every window has a box of luxuriant foliage and flowering plants. But every house can be made suitable for the culture of at least a few choice plants.

Growing plants can be used in many ways for home decoration and nowadays a house, if ever so costly, looks poor and tasteless without their proper use. Mantel-pieces, shelves, pieces of furniture, stands, tables, and cupboards, all offer some suitable place for ornamental plants.

Many people decorate their rooms with artificial plants— senseless caricatures of the real things. It can only be said that this shows an extremely bad taste and a hankering after outward show. The real plant, when unfolding leaf after leaf and blossom after blossom is not merely a beautiful object, it is a living being replete with interest; for it is not only the form we admire or the color, but more than anything the mystery of life, the wonderful and constant changes working beneath our eyes.

Whether plants have any influence on the health of persons living in rooms where they are grown, or not, is a matter of conjecture only. In ordinary, well-ventilated houses there is no need of plants to purify the atmosphere, nor is there any danger to be apprehended from their use. Strong odors, whether arising from plants or other sources, may be injurious to sensitive persons, but very few flowers, likely to be cultivated in a dwelling-room, are as strongly scented as that.

We may therefore safely conclude that plants can do no injury to the health of anybody ; but, on the other hand, as they brighten the home and give diversity and interest to the most lonely place, their influence for good, in one way at least, is beyond all doubt.

To begin in the right way always saves trouble and annoyance in the end. Cheap, overgrown, and sickly plants peddled in the streets are expensive at any price, and will as a rule give more trouble than pleasure. The stock, to begin with, should be absolutely healthy, whether it be seeds or plants. It is far better to spend a little more money for first-class material than to buy cheap things that are unsightly in the beginning and almost sure to die.

Many soft-wooded plants, when once on hand, are easily increased, and most such plants should be frequently renewed by means of cuttings, and there should be no hesitancy in throwing away old worthless and unsightly stuff.

At present plants of all kinds are comparatively cheap. Even Orchids, the noblest of flowers, can be obtained at very low prices, considering the difficulty with which they are gathered and imported from far-away countries. Hundreds of thousands of Palms are raised annually in this country for home-decoration, and good plants of the best kinds can be bought for very little. For those of limited means there are numerous cheaper but not less beautiful kinds of plants. Many beautiful plants can be raised from seeds or grown from bulbs or tubers offered for sale by most seedsmen.

Very little work, but considerable thoughtfulness is needed to make a success of everything. Cleanliness is very important in the treatment of plants. Careful watering is another thing to be observed, as some plants evaporate in a single day a quantity of water many times their own weight. These would soon wither and die if they were neglected for any length of time. Anybody interested in plants and watching their silent development will soon learn to discern their need. Almost imperceptible changes in the color of the foliage will tell if the plants need more nutriment, or if they need more water or less. Too much water as a rule brings a yellow tint to the leaves; insufficient nutriment will cause a dull appearance easily perceived by an experienced eye. Want of water may bring insects or stop the growth of an otherwise healthy plant.

If a good selection is made a constant supply of flowers can be had all the year long. The most suitable ones for winter flowering are the many kinds of bulbous plants which are so easy to obtain and easy to force. Hyacinths, Narcissi, Lilies, Lily of the Valley, and others equally beautiful, are among the best flowers to be had. Then again, many shrubby plants bloom either constantly, as the many varieties of Begonia semperflorens, or during the better part of winter as many kinds of Orchids, Begonias, Chrysanthemums and other florists' flowers. The spring, summer, and autumn flowers are abundant. In early spring the golden Cytisus opens its fragrant flowers. The many-colored Azaleas are gay with blossoms. Cape Heaths continue to bloom, and Primulas, Cinerarias, and other well-known plants are at their best. In summer suitable flowering-plants are very numerous. For fall and winter, Chrysanthemums, Roses, Carnations, and Persian Violets cannot be excelled.

We may, therefore, safely say that there is no pleasure so

profitable and instructive as the simple art of window gardening. With some thoughtfulness, judicious selection of plants, light and proper apartments, and the glorious climate which nature has provided for us, our homes need not lack the glad presence of green foliage and fragrant flowers.

PART I

PROPAGATION AND CARE OF HOUSE PLANTS

I

THE PLANT

MOST plants familiar to us grow from seeds. The germ, swelling under the influence of heat and moisture, gradually bursts the seed, the little root descends in the soil, and the primary leaves expand in the air.

Seeds are of different kinds: some contain a horn-like substance called albumen, in which the germ or embryo lies imbedded; others are entirely filled by the cotyledons or seed-lobes of a fully developed plant. When the embryo is very small and the albumen fills the entire seed, the germination is generally slow and more uncertain than when the fully developed plant has merely to straighten out and grow, as in the common maple. The baby plants derive their first nutriment from the stored-up matter in the fleshy seed-leaves or the abundant albumen, but soon assimilate food taken up in the ordinary way from soil and air.

The root, gradually branching, penetrates the soil in all directions, and by means of numerous exceedingly fine hairs just above the growing-point, absorbs nutriment dissolved in water. This nutriment and water ascends as sap to the leaves where, under the action of heat and light, it is assimilated and becomes available as food. Roots are very different in shape and quality. Some are almost hair-like, white and delicate; others are

woody or fleshy.   Fleshy roots, as the root of the common
Dahlia, serve to store up plant-food for future use, and plants
so provided for are generally natives of dry and arid regions.
Aërial roots are found in many Orchids, Ferns, and plants of
the Pine-apple family.   These are usually fleshy and seldom
branched ; they absorb nutriment from the moisture-laden
atmosphere.   Roots of pot-plants, if over-fed or over-watered,
are apt to sicken and decay ; hence a thorough drainage and
judicious watering are absolutely necessary to keep such plants
healthy and vigorous.

The stem is herbaceous, as in most of our summer-flowers,
or woody, as in trees and shrubs.   The woody stem grows year
after year, increasing in girth by means of yearly deposits of
wood below the bark.   The herbaceous stem is annual, pro-
ceeding from a seed or from a perennial root or an underground stem.   The rhizome is a creeping stem generally
growing below the ground.   Rhizomes are often mistaken for
roots, but the difference lies in the fact that roots produce no
buds.   All underground parts of a plant producing buds and
shoots are therefore stems.   The Lily of the Valley, the
Waterflag, and many other familiar plants have fleshy root-like
stems.   Corms and tubers are short, fleshy stems, not unlike
bulbs in appearance and serving the same purpose, but differ
by not being composed of scales and layers as are all bulbs.
Gladiolus and Crocus are common examples.   In Cactus and
other succulent plants, the stem becomes very thick and fleshy,
and is generally leafless.   The green epidermis of such stems
serves the same purpose as foliage of other plants.

The stem sometimes becomes long and slender, winding round
different objects for support, or climbing by means of tendrils.
Such plants are called vines, creepers, or twining-plants.

PLATE I.

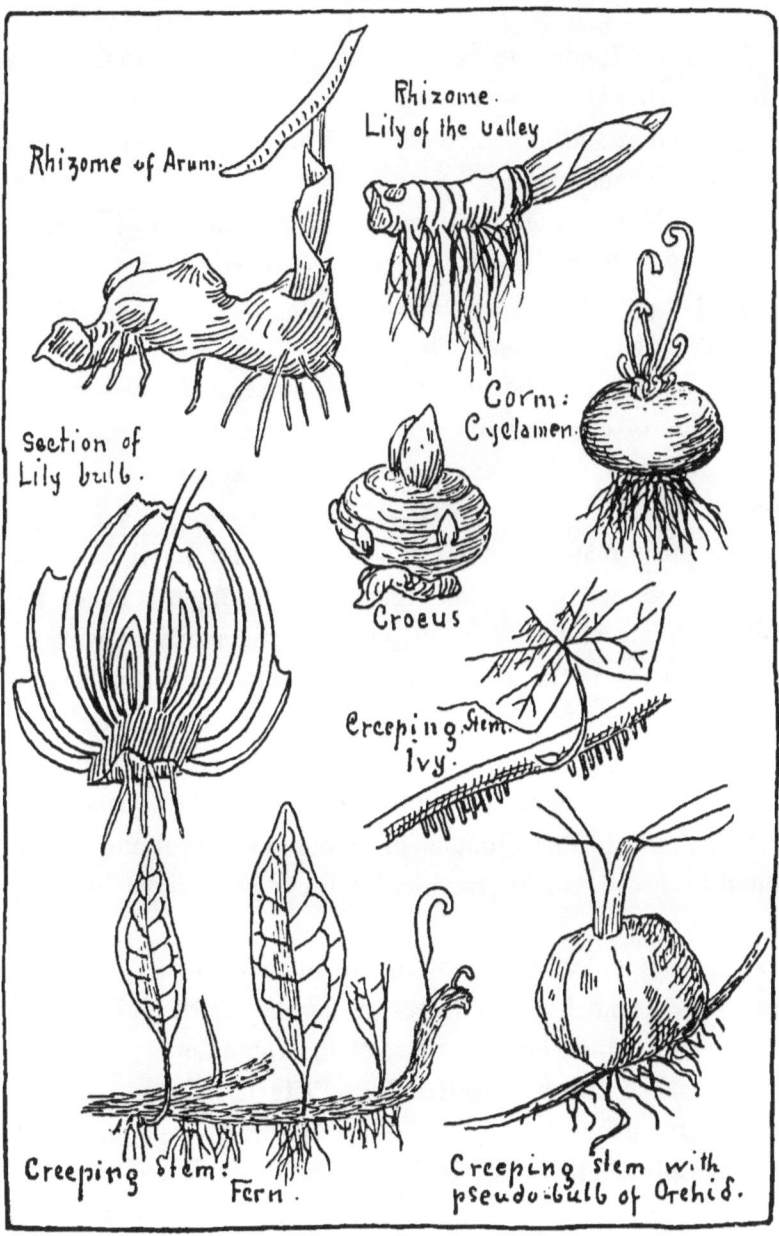

Rhizome of Arum.

Rhizome.
Lily of the valley

Section of
Lily bulb.

Corm:
Cyclamen.

Croeus

Creeping Stem.
Ivy.

Creeping stem: Fern.

Creeping stem with
pseudo-bulb of Orchid.

Roots and Rhizomes.

Buds are formations of the stem; from these come leaves and branches and flowers. In deciduous plants the buds are very different and more complex than in evergreens, being protected by recinous scales.

All bulbs are merely buds composed of a number of more or less fleshy scales or leaves. They serve to store up nutriment or for the purpose of propagation.

Leaves serve to assimilate plant-food under the action of light and heat. The under side of the leaf is covered with thousands of openings through which the carbonic acid of the air is absorbed. The leaves also serve as organs of evaporation.

The green matter of the leaf is called chlorophyll, and can only be formed under the influence of sunlight; hence the yellowish or white leaves of plants accidentally growing in deep shade. As the leaf is one of the most important organs of the plant and absolutely necessary to growth and development, it is important always to keep the same clean and in a healthy state. Leaves are either simple, as in the Oleander, or compound as in the Mimosæ, or sometimes absent and substituted by broad and flattened leaf-stalks or petioles, as in many Acacias.

The simple leaves are of many different forms; the chief types are parallel-veined leaves, as in the Calla, and all lilies and netted-veined ones, as those of the Geranium.

The shape differs considerably. Plate II. gives an idea of the most common types. The edge of a leaf is seldom entire. When only slightly cut, it is toothed or crenate; or, when wavy as that of the oak, undulate. According to the degree of incision it is called cut, lobed, cleft, parted, or divided; divided being the highest degree of incision. Next to these come com-

PLATE II.

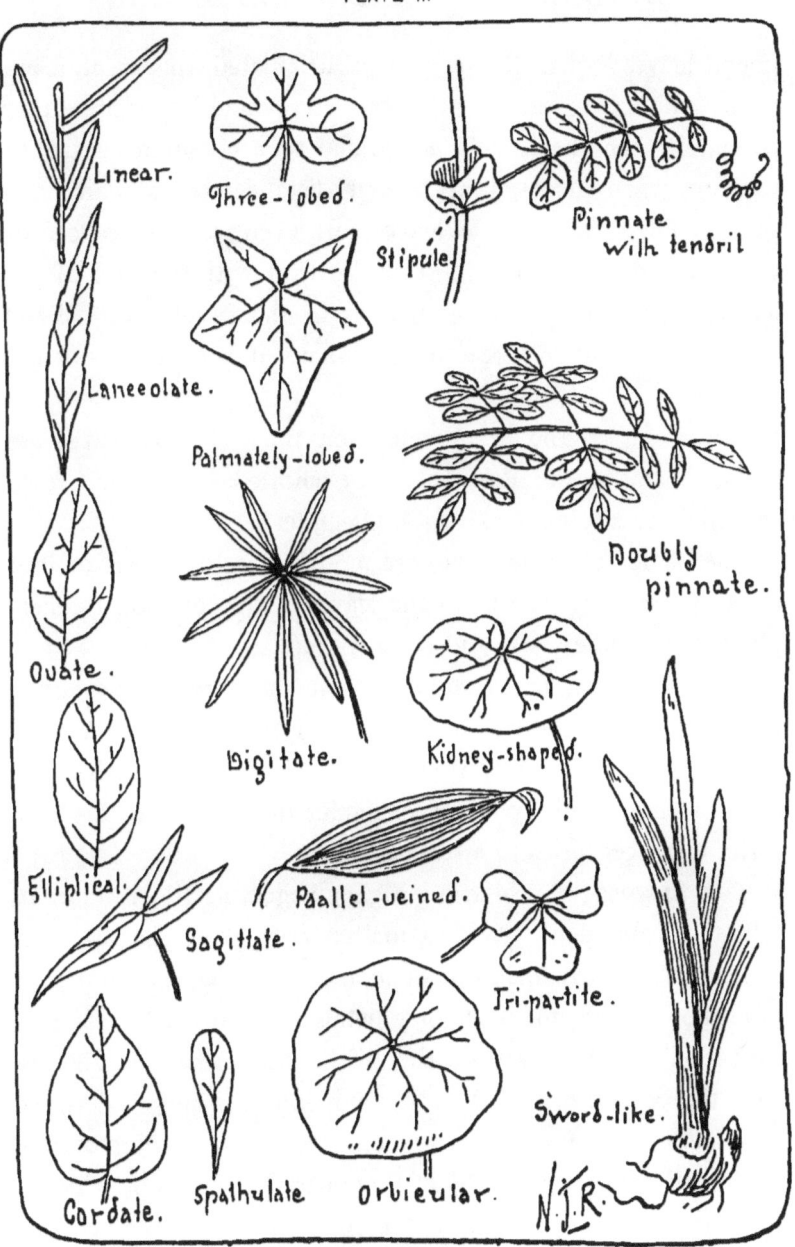

Linear.

Three-lobed.

Stipule.

Pinnate
with tendril

Lanceolate.

Palmately-lobed.

Doubly
pinnate.

Ovate.

Digitate.

Kidney-shaped.

Elliptical.

Parallel-veined.

Sagittate.

Tri-partite.

Sword-like.

Cordate.

Spathulate

Orbicular.

N.J.R.

Simple and Compound Leaves.

pound leaves; when the segment is articulated, that is, attached to the whole by means of a joint.   Compound leaves are either palmate, when the leaflets are joined to a common centre, or pinnate, when disposed at regular distances on a main leaf-stalk.   There are pinnate leaves with even pairs of leaflets, or with an odd one at the tip of the leaf, or with the end of the leaflet converted into a tendril, as in the sweet pea.   When a leaf is doubly or three times pinnate, it is called bi- or tri-pinnate.

According to the arrangement on the stem the leaves are opposite, as in the Periwinkle, or whorled, as in the Crown Imperial, or alternate, as in the Oleander.

The blades of some leaves are modified into pitchers or into traps for catching insects, as the leaves of the common Pitcher-plant, the Saddle-wort, and the Fly-trap.

Some leaves are fleshy and succulent, and serve for storage in the same way as fleshy stems or roots in other plants.   A common example is the American Aloe.   Many plants of this class have dry and leathery leaves engendered by exposure for cen turies upon centuries to a tropical sun.

The flowers, in which all higher vegetable life reaches its fullest development, are, no matter how great the apparent difference, formed upon one general plan.   The essential parts of all flowers are not the showy petals, but the small, insignifi-cant-looking organs within, the pistil and stamens.   The pis-til is the central organ, the lower portion of which is destined to develop into fruit ; the stamens are the fertilizing organs. The pistil consists generally of three parts : the *ovary*, which is the lower part and contains the rudimentary seeds, the *style*, and the *stigma*.   The style may be absent, but the stigma which receives the pollen from the anthers, and the ovary, are

PLATE III.

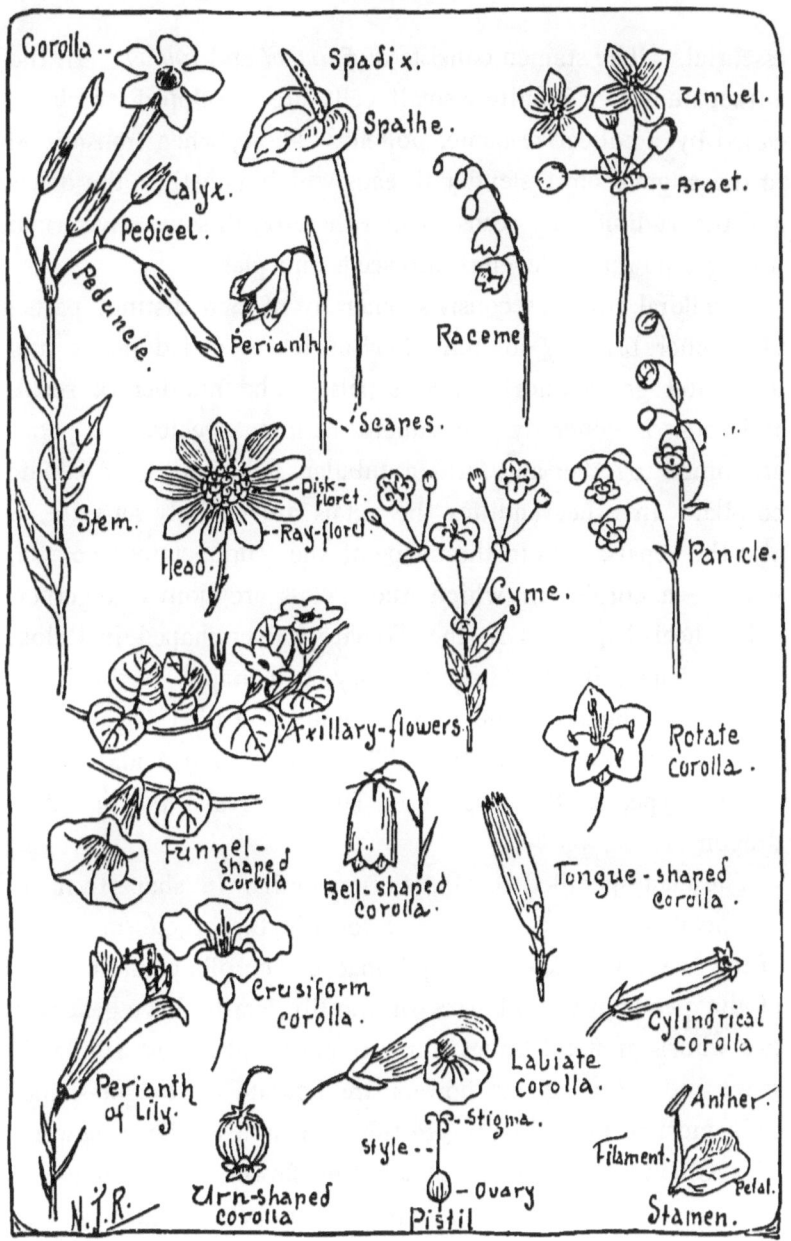

Flowers and Inflorescence.

essential. The stamen consists of *filament* and *anther*. In the anther numerous infinitely small cells are developed which are called by a collective name, pollen. These, when transmitted to the stigma, emit slender threads which penetrate the ovary and the rudimentary seeds, which thereby, in some mysterious way, get power to develop into seeds and plants.

The floral envelope consists generally of two distinct parts: One inner brightly colored whorl of leaves called petals, and one outer green whorl called sepals. The number of sepals and petals is generally the same. In some species the petals are joined together and form a tubular, bell-shaped, or labiate corolla. In other families the petals are entirely separate, as also the sepals. As to the shape of the gamopetalous corolla, that is, a corolla in which the petals are joined together, it is wheel-shaped, as in the Tomato, salver-shaped in Phlox, funnel-shaped in the Morning-glory, bell-shaped in the Hare-bell, and tubular in the now common so-called Cigar-plant, and in the common Heaths. There are also irregular shapes of this type, as the ringent or labiate corolla of the Snap-dragon.

The many-petalled corolla is often similar in shape to many one-petalled flowers. A special form is the cruciform corolla of the Wallflower and the papilionaceous corolla of most plants of the pea-family. Flowers of the lily family have generally two whorls of floral leaves, three in each and almost similar in shape and color. Some flowers are ligulate or tongue-shaped as in most plants belonging to the aster family. The "flower" of a Chrysanthemum is not a single flower, but a collection or *head* of numerous flowers with a monopetalous strap-shaped corolla. At the same time the central flowers, in most species of Chrysanthemums, Asters, and their allies are always tubular.

Double flowers are artificial productions obtained through intense culture. In these the essential parts have developed into colored petals; for this reason most double flowers produce no fruit. In Orchids the flowers are of a peculiar shape, all the essential parts being joined together and dependent upon insects for fertilization. The flowers are sometimes protected by colored bracts or spathes, as in the case of the common Calla. With regard to the inflorescence, flowers are generally produced together: in *racemes* when stalked and springing from one main stem or peduncle; in *corymbs* when the flowers, disposed one above the other on a main peduncle, form a flat cluster; in *umbells* when the pedicels spring from a common point; in *spikes* when the flowers of a raceme are sessile. The flowers of the Calla are collected in a fleshy spike and protected by a showy leaf called *spathe*. Many compositions of these original types are found. Flowers are sometimes produced singly from the axis of leaves, and are then said to be axillary. In Plate II. the most common types of flowers and flower-clusters are illustrated.

The fruit is sometimes as ornamental as the flower, but a superficial glance at fruits and seeds is all that can be spared. As flowers are simply modified branches, so the different parts of a flower are only modified leaves. Even the most altered parts, viz., the stamens and pistils, are simply modifications of the green parts of the plant. The fruit consists, therefore, of one or more altered leaves joined together and enclosing one or more seeds. This is most apparent in such types as the Pea and Bean, or in the carpel of a Pæony. In berries and stone-fruits all parts are greatly modified. A fruit is anything containing one or more seeds, from the dry capsule of a flax-plant to the succulent product of a water-melon. The seed is the essential part, to the production of which the life of the plant has been devoted from its germination.

Ferns and clubmosses are flowerless plants, reproduced by spores which in the case of ferns are collected in fruit spots on the back of the leaves, or bordering the edge, or disposed in capsules at the termination of veins. The spores retain their power of growth longer than any seeds. In growing, a small flat body is formed, on which the organs, corresponding to pistil and anther in flowering plants, develop. These are always disposed on the lower side of this flat body or prothallium and, fertilized in due course, give rise each to a small plant, which in its first stage is very delicate.

The leaves of Ferns and Palms and Sagopalms are called fronds. They are mostly of a luxurious growth, of elegant habit, and very ornamental.

A curious process of reproduction is noted in many ferns, by means of buds forming on the back of the frond, which develop into entire plants, and when planted carefully facilitate the propagation of some of our most beautiful ferns.

APPLIANCES

 FEW special appliances may be of great use to the grower who is altogether confined within the house, who has no garden or place for frames or pits. In his case some arrangement for keeping a little soil and manure in a proper way should be made. A good, strong wooden box with special departments for the various kinds of soils and manures, and also one for pots, watering-cans, sponges, sprayers, etc., would be very useful. This could easily be kept in the cellar or any other out-of-the way place where potting, cleaning, and other rough work could be done. One or two sieves and a few shallow boxes for carrying soil, for potting and for shifting plants, ought to be kept, as also a spade for mixing soil. A sufficient number of pots in all sizes, and a few shallow pans for propagating, should always be handy. A good watering-pot of the flat approved pattern, not too large for using in a room, and for spraying foliage a Scollay bulb, which can be used in any room without moistening carpets or furniture. A small brass hand-

Watering Can with Rose.

Scollay Bulb.

syringe is required for large plants, if a green-house or pit is kept. For cleaning purposes a few small soft sponges and a bottle of fir-tree oil are better than anything else. Fir-tree oil, while a good thorough insecticide, is at the same time agreeable to handle and efficient for cleaning the foliage of palms and other plants that can easily be washed. Sticks, if possible green-painted ones, these being neater, and Raffia bast for tying should not be omitted, as these materials may be required unexpectedly.

For propagating, any good sharp pocket-knife will do. For tender plants and for plants that require very moist air, there is nothing better than neat glass cases that can be made in any size with a movable top and zinc bottom. In such boxes the atmosphere can be kept moist by spraying, and the temperature equable by means of shading from strong sun and ventilating. For tender ferns, clubmosses, young seedlings of Begonias, etc., these are necessary.

It will be seen that these requisites are not difficult to supply. Ordinary wooden boxes with a lid will do for the soil. Everything else can be obtained through any florist or seedsman for a mere trifle.

Pots of porous material are better than heavy ornamental ones. The surplus water will evaporate with greater ease and the air has freer access to soil and roots ; both matters of great importance.

For many small plants which form beautiful masses of leaves and flowers, such as Gloxinias, Achimenes, and many bulbs, low pots commonly known as *pans*, can be used with advantage. Many kinds of ferns can also be grown in these. Hanging-baskets of earthenware are easier to use than wire or wooden baskets. These and square blocks of cork or wood are used for many Orchids and Bromeliads.

SOILS AND MANURES

oam. Good fibrous loam, obtained by cutting sods in a rich pasture or by the wayside, when well decayed, is the best and cleanest soil that can be had for general purposes. It can be obtained, ready for mixing, of any florist. This can be made up to suit most plants by mixing with clean silver-sand and decayed manure or leaf-mould, or in some cases with peat, as directed in the special chapters on plants.

Leaf Mould consists of decayed leaves and twigs of deciduous trees. It is found in woods and forests or made up by allowing heaps of leaves to rot gradually. This soil, when sifted, is very useful for mixing with loam for a number of greenhouse-plants, and is especially useful for seedlings and cuttings.

Peat is found in swamps and bogs, and is formed of decayed bog-plants, the fibrous and decayed parts of ferns and mosses, and is a very light and porous soil, deficient in mineral substances, but suitable for ferns, orchids, and plants of the Pineapple family, as also, when decayed and sifted, for mixing in soils for many soft-wooded plants, such as Begonia and Primulas. It is also required for the Azalea and Camellia.

Sand. If possible, clean white silver-sand or coarse sand from a river-shore must be had for making up light soils for bulbs, cuttings, seeds, and a number of plants. It is indispensable for propagation and for storing bulbs and tuberous roots during their period of rest.

Cow Manure is the best natural fertilizer obtainable. When well decayed and cleaned it is not at all objectionable to handle. Ordinary good soil, when mixed with this and a trifle of bone-dust, contains all the nutriment required by the great majority of plants.

Horse Manure cannot be used for pot-plants until well decayed and of the appearance of black humus-rich soil. In this state it can be used in quantity for Fuchsias, Geraniums, and similar plants. About one-fourth, with one-half good loam and a fourth part of sand, makes a very good soil for ordinary use.

Poultry, Sheep, and Pigeon Droppings, when pulverized, are clean to handle and make very strong fertilizers for top-dressing and liquid manures for Palms and foliage plants. They should be used moderately, a thin layer barely covering the surface of the soil is sufficient.

Bone Dust is a safe and durable ingredient in soils for strong-growing plants, for Roses, Chrysanthemums, and many other vigorous things. It can be used in the proportion of two or three parts to a hundred parts of soil.

Many kinds of fertilizers specially prepared for house-plants, and sold under different names by seedsmen and florists, are clean and scentless and suit the purpose very well. Some of the best are commonly sold in packages with directions for use, and as a rule these can be relied on.

All soils when used should be moderately moist and agreeable to the touch. To preserve the soil in this state it should be kept in boxes covered with a lid. It is necessary to keep it pure and clean, and to mix only what is needed at a time. Should the soil be too dry it must be watered beforehand, so as to be suitable for use when needed. If too wet it must be allowed to dry until satisfactory.

Soils for foliage plants should be rich and must contain plenty of ammonia, which is an ingredient in most natural manure. Soil for large plants should be lumpy and fibrous, and sifted soil should be used only for seedlings, cuttings, or delicate plants. Most of these varieties of soils can be obtained through any first-class florist. The window-gardener who wants to be exact and careful had, however, better mix for himself any special soil that will be recommended later on in the cultural notes. Soils and manures in small quantities should always be kept on hand in boxes, tubs, or other convenient receptacles, or, as recommended in the chapter on appliances, in a specially provided box.

PROPAGATION

ANY plants can be profitably propagated by cuttings in a window with no exceptional care or skill. Among these are most quick-growing soft-wooded plants: Pelargoniums, Geraniums, Fuchsias, Marguerites, Begonias, Chrysanthemums, Carnations, and Roses yield to a patient endeavor. Many plants can also be grown from seeds with great ease, and one of the greatest pleasures of window-gardening is certainly to watch the development of quick-growing plants from the embryo. Cinerarias, Calceolarias, German Stocks, Chinese Primulas, and Wallflowers all grow with the greates* of ease.

Cuttings or slips are made in different ways according to the nature of the wood. Soft-wooded cuttings are made of young growing, half ripened shoots with one or more leaves. For an example, take a brittle shoot of a Verbena with about six fully developed leaves, remove the three lower ones with a sharp knife and shorten the remaining ones slightly. Some soft-wooded cuttings require bottom heat, and can therefore not be successfully rooted in a room. Others, and chiefly those of greenhouse plants, require no bottom heat. Hard-wood cuttings take a considerable time to root and cannot, except in a few cases, be rooted in a window. All plants that cannot be prop-

PLATE IV.

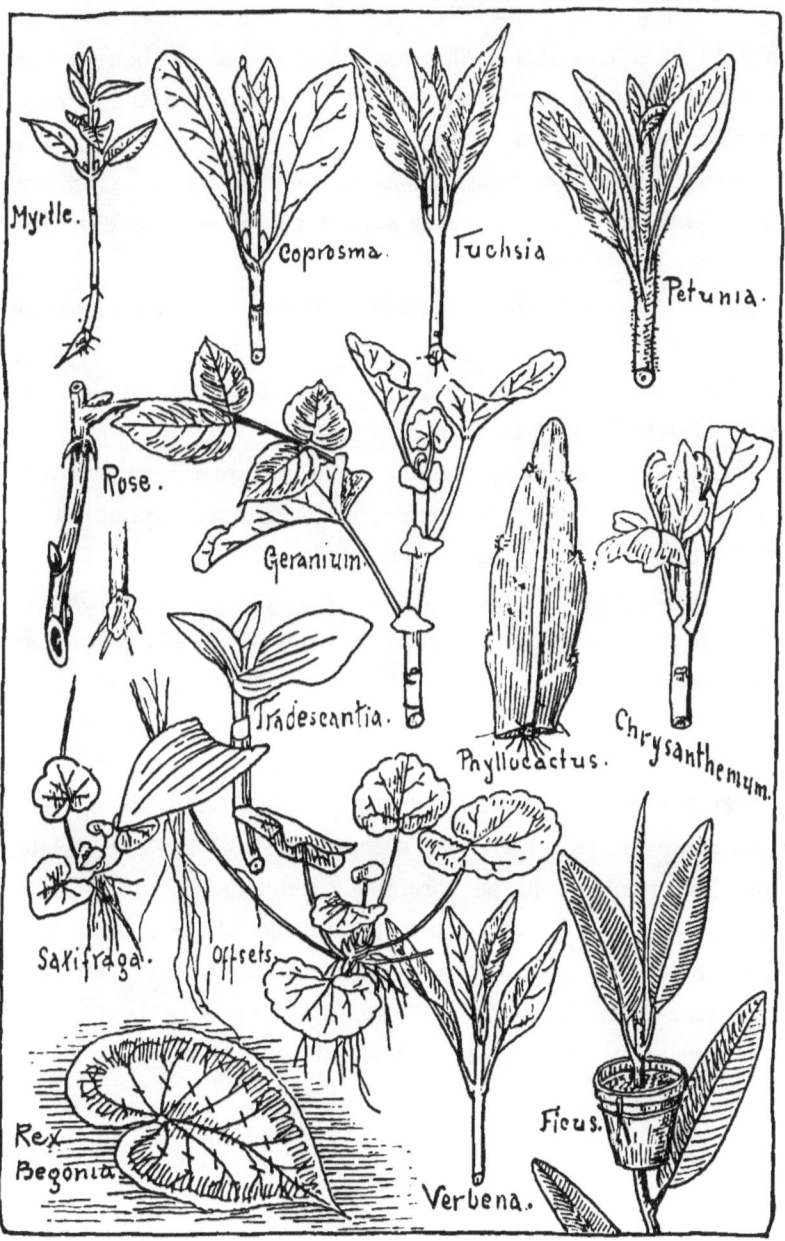

Cuttings.

agated with ease in a room or window should be bought from a florist to save time and money. Cuttings root in various ways. Some form a cellular mass where the branch has been separated, which is called *cambium* or *callus,* and make roots from this point only. Others root below every eye or from any part below ground.

Rose cuttings should be made with two or three eyes, and the end should be cut obliquely below the lowest eye. Cuttings of Geraniums, Fuchsias, etc., require less care. Carnation cuttings should be split in their lower ends.

Leaf Cuttings are pieces of leaves with one or more strong veins that root readily in sand. Rex-Begonias, Bryophyllums, and Gloxinias are propagated in this manner.

If the cuttings are made; a shallow pan or pot should be well drained by means of pieces of broken pots and some rough soil, and finally filled with sharp, clean silver-sand. This should be moderately moist when used and must be pressed down quite firmly. In the case of easily rooted plants the cuttings can be inserted all over the surface of the pot, but some cuttings root best when placed in contact with the wall of the pot. After insertion they should be carefully watered, must never be allowed to get too dry or too wet, and should be shaded from the strong sun, and according to their nature be kept in a moderate heat. When the cuttings are known to be of more than ordinary value, or if difficult to root, allow room at the surface to cover with a piece of clean glass.

The seed is the most natural means of reproduction, and many plants can be raised in this way by almost anybody. Seeds should be covered according to their size, and very fine seeds must be sown on the surface of the soil in specially prepared pots, covered with a glass and shaded until germination, and must never be allowed to dry. Too much moisture may also cause the seeds to decay, especially if somewhat old.

Many plants are easily propagated by division. Bulbous-rooted plants are more particularly apt to be increased in that way.

Wardian Glass Case for Propagation and for Tender Plants.

The reader is asked to study carefully the illustrations to this chapter on Plate IV., and to note all reference to the propagation of each variety in the articles on plants. It is, however, not advisable to attempt too much, it being wiser to grow plants already on hand into fine specimens than to try propagation. Young plants of all leading varieties are generally cheap, and if propagation is attempted it should be done more for the pleasure of the thing than for any other consideration.

POTTING

WHEN the young cutting is well rooted it should be transferred from the sand to ordinary soil, and according to its nature be potted more or less firmly. All truly woody plants require a firm potting from the beginning, and often die by the wholesale if potted too loosely. Soft-wooded plants, on the other hand, do better in less firm soil, while seedlings of such plants as Primulas, Gloxinias, and Begonias can be potted quite loosely. Young cuttings and seedlings should never be given too large pots. Success depends largely on the observation of this rule. For rapid-growing, soft-wooded, or herbaceous plants frequent repotting is necessary until the plants reach normal size and are ready for flowering. In potting and repotting care must be taken to

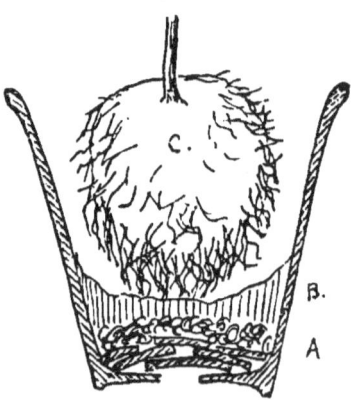

Diagram showing Pot Ready for Potting. A, drainage; B, soil; C, root-ball of plant prepared for potting.

preserve all good roots and to insert them in as natural a position as possible; no roots should be bent or bruised in the operation. In repotting plants already established in pots, place the left hand carefully over the top of the soil, two fingers on each side of the plant, reverse it, and with a sharp knock by the rim of the pot on some hard object remove the clump from the pot. If it is well rooted and in good condition, and it is desirable to give more pot-room, remove only the loose soil from the top-edge and the crocks from the bottom ; loosen the roots gently and then plant in a well-drained pot. Hard-wooded plants must be potted quite firmly, while soft-wooded ones do best in moderately loose soil. For potting large plants a pointed stick is required to push the soil down to the roots. In this case place a small quantity of soil in the bottom, put the clump down, throw some soil loosely about it and knock the pot slightly, first with one side of the bottom, then with the other to shake down the soil among the roots, holding the plant in the right place at the same time. Then fill in the remainder and finish off more or less firmly according to the nature of the plant. The pots should, when finished, never be quite full, allowing a liberal space for watering. After potting, a good soaking is always given with a rose. Potting in a house can be done in a cellar, and no special bench is required.

Drainage is necessary for most plants. Some require more, others less. For some Orchids, Ferns, and plants of the Pineapple family the pots are more than half filled with broken crocks. In draining, place a large flat potsherd over the hole in the bottom and then place a few others round it for ordinary potting. If the plant is known to suffer easily from too damp soil, throw a number of small ones in on the top and cover up with coarse siftings, fibres, or a very little moss.

The pots must always be clean inside and out when used, and should be examined so as to ascertain that the outlet for water is satisfactory. If the plants have been much disturbed by potting they should be shaded for a few days after.

Bulbs for forcing should be potted in the autumn months. Lilies require about six-inch pots. Freesias, Tulips, and Crocus should be put several together, Hyacinths singly, and Narcissi three or five together according to size. For further directions the reader is referred to the pages on these plants. In potting bulbs the soil should not be packed, but simply shaken down, the top of the bulb always being left immediately below the surface. A good thorough watering or two successive ones must be given after potting, and the pots should be placed in a dark, cool place until rooted, when they should be placed in brisk heat in the warmest place the house affords and kept shaded until sprouting, when they may be gradually removed to light. In planting hardy plants from the ground or from the woods, good specimens should always be chosen, taken with a clump, and put into as small pots as possible without injury to the roots. Hardy plants are very good subjects for winter-flowering. The Christmas Rose, the Japanese Spirea, several native Orchids and Ferns, Anemones, and hosts of others, are both easy to grow and highly decorative in a room.

Orchids and Bromeliads must be potted in a special way in well-drained pots or baskets, in a mixture of sphagnum moss and fibrous lumps of peat. In repotting Orchids, remove the plant carefully from the pot or basket, pick off all old decaying material, fill the pot partly with alternate lumps of peat and moss, put the roots in their place, and fill in the material firmly so as to leave the plant upright in the middle, slightly raised above the rim of the pot. The surface should then be trimmed clean by means of a pair of ordinary shears.

In filling hanging baskets or vases with an assortment of

plants the stronger ones should always be placed in the centre, first of all. Then a circle or two of flowering and foliage-plants with trailing vines to hang gracefully over the rim. The room between the clumps should be filled in with good soil and firmly packed without disturbing the roots.

Window-boxes before planting should be lined with zinc to prevent the wood from rotting. The edges should be covered with low trailing plants. No drainage is needed, as the box will be exposed to wind and sun and consequently dries quickly.

VI

FORCING

THIS is a process by which hardy plants are brought into flower by means of artificial heat and moisture in a close green-house or other place, during the winter months. Hardy perennial plants and shrubs are very suitable for this purpose, even some of our native wild flowers make admirable subjects. The way to proceed is simplicity itself. The plants should be taken up with as good roots as possible; the clump must be carefully reduced and potted firmly in as small pots as possible. They should then be thoroughly watered and placed in a shady frame, and covered with soil or leaves until rooted. Some species, in fact most hardy ones, must be allowed to freeze before forcing. After this they should be introduced for a few days into brisk heat, when they can be grown naturally until flowering. Where there is a greenhouse or pit, forcing can be done admirably without any extra outlay. If it be desired to grow a few hardy plants for winter bloom where there is no such convenience, the problem is more difficult, and should not be attempted on any large scale. Hardy Ferns, however, taken from the wood need no special care in forcing, and can simply be grown in an ordinary window. So also plants that naturally bloom during the winter months or in very early spring, as the Christmas Rose, the Eranthis, and the little blue Anemone. The foliage of plants of this class should be kept quite moist until the flowers begin to expand.

Hyacinths can be forced in clean water in narrow vases, made on purpose. The lower surface of the bulb should merely touch the water. If kept in a moderately warm room, roots will soon fill the vase. A shady position is necessary until the scape has grown to a height of about six inches. The Chinese Sacred Lily, a kind of Narcissus with large bulbs, may be grown in a similar manner in glass bowls, half-filled with clean pebbles of about the size of a hazel-nut. The bowl should be partly filled with water and one or two large bulbs placed in the centre. These soon commence to root, and flower in about a month or six weeks. The Chinese Sacred Lily, when grown in this way, is both interesting and ornamental.

VII

WATERING

WATERING must be considered with due regard to the nature of the plant under treatment. A Cactus or other succulent plant requires less water than robust-foliage plants, and while a slight neglect in watering a Cactus would be of no consequence, the neglect of a Fern in full growth might do great injury. The soil should in no case be kept continually wet, but merely sufficiently moist to insure a satisfactory growth. Watering can be almost entirely dispensed with during the winter months with many slow-growing Cactaceæ, but most plants require more or less water all the year round. On a sunny summer day more water is of course needed than in the dull season of the year. The amount of water taken up by healthy foliage-plants during a hot summer day is sometimes quite surprising. One way to ascertain if a plant is dry is by tapping the pot by the hand, when if dry it will give a ringing sound. But the amateur will soon learn to discover the dry ones merely by looking at the soil.

Water should, if possible, be soft. Rain-water collected for the purpose is the best for ordinary use. Palms and other foliage-plants require spraying every day in dry weather, or where this is impracticable the plants should be gone over once in a while with a moist sponge, an operation which need not be tedious or of long duration. Special care should be taken in spraying and watering cuttings and young seedlings. Seedlings in particular are apt to "damp off" if the soil is unduly dry and the top too moist. Watering of delicate seedlings must be done with great care with a Scollay bulb or with a very fine rose. In America watering can hardly be overdone in the summer time. Provided the plants are well drained, they should be watered every day in bright weather— study the nature of your plants and the nature of the weather, and you will soon know the path that leads to success.

A number of plants require a full or partial rest during winter. Nearly all bulbous plants and corms can be dried off as soon as the season's growth is over, and from such plants water should be withdrawn gradually when the foliage begins to show signs of ripening. Most plants should be kept slightly dryer during the winter months. Tropical plants kept in too low a temperature should also be kept rather dry until a higher temperature makes it possible for them to recommence activity. Too much water for plants exposed to cold will cause sickness and decay. On the other hand, neglect of watering during the extreme heat of summer will invariably bring insects and diseases. If the pots are not protected against sun and wind, no watering will be sufficient to keep up a growing moisture.

VIII

CLEANING

CLEANING plants when infested with insects or covered with dust liable to interfere with the normal action of the leaf, or if slightly attacked by disease. is a most important work. It does not entail any considerable loss of time or shifting of plants, for it can be neatly and easily done even in a window.

If the plants are infested with scales or mealy bugs the work is somewhat tedious, owing to the necessity of removing every visible enemy by means of a pointed stick if the sponge cannot reach it. For general use, fir-tree oil is a very cleanly and efficient insecticide. It should be mixed according to the directions on each bottle. It has the advantage over others in not injuring the hands; it will leave even a white hand much whiter.

Even when cleaning is not absolutely needed for any apparent reason, it is useful as a preventive against both insects and diseases. Sponges used for washing plants must be soft and free from any granular matter or sand, which is apt to scratch the surface of the leaves. When the foliage is too small to be washed leaf by leaf, an immersion in a weak solution of fir-tree oil will be useful.

If large foliage-plants such as Palms, Rubber-trees, and Dracenas are merely dusty, a good rubbing of the foliage with a soft cloth will make the leaves clean and glossy. This method is better than washing when the plants are absolutely healthy and free from insects. Cleanliness will do more to keep them away than all remedies. Every lady desirous of growing plants successfully should bear this in mind. Not only should the leaves be kept free from dust and other objectionable matter, but pots, vases, urns, and baskets must have a similar attention.

The purpose of window and parlor gardening being an æsthetic one, anything that will heighten the general effect should be done, and cleanliness is one of the great foundations of all truly æsthetic enjoyment.

IX

SPECIAL WINDOWS AND TERRARIUMS

ANY plants require for their full development a moister and more equable atmosphere than an ordinary dwelling-house can offer. Such plants should rather be excluded from a collection than be brought to a place where they are sure in the long run to be anything but ornamental. But persons who would like to grow any variety of this kind can, in an easy and inexpensive way, provide a suitable place for such plants. A good bay-window, or any spacious light and wide window, should be selected for this purpose, and separated from the room proper by means of glass doors, leaving an ample space in which a special atmospheric condition can be maintained by means of daily sprayings of the foliage. Being more close and easily over-heated on sunny days, facilities for airing and shading should be maintained and the temperature should be kept as equal as possible. In such a small enclosure the plants should be arranged on stands and brackets, and some, satisfied with less sun, even on the floor. This little mimic conservatory should not be overcrowded ; a few good specimens of the best kinds, of exceptionally beautiful Ferns, Clubmosses, Palms, and Orchids, that would suffer in the room itself, should be all, for it must be here borne in mind that an unusual number of all kinds and conditions of plants, arranged in a greenhouse-like way, would be extremely bad taste and not likely to give any special pleasure.

Terrariums, or large glass cases on stands, can be provided for the same purpose and are more suitable for small and deli-

Terrarium.

cate plants, such as filmy Ferns, some Clubmosses, a few rare Aroids and Gesneraceæ. Such cases can be tastefully made of wood, polished or otherwise, or with marble base and plate-glass sides and cover, and can in themselves be rendered really ornamental objects. Supposing a terrarium of this description ready for use; we will first build little rockeries by means of loose sand-stones, here higher, there lower, with a gradual slope from the middle to the sides. Here and there in this fundamental structure leave larger and smaller fissures that can be filled with suitable soil. We now select some of the most beautiful plants that can be found. A few especially fine Aroideæ with glossy many-colored foliage; a Fittonia with silvery- or golden-veined leaves to hang over an edge here, some trailing Tradescantias there or the white-striped Panicum, a beautiful grass. A red-fruited Nertera will look well on the edge close to the glass, while a small and slender palm, the Cocos Weddeliana may rise from a mass of Adiantums or some other delicate-leaved fern. We may also have a few decaying branches of birch or oak covered with the hair-like masses of some filmy fern and rich and vigorous upright-growing Club-mosses among a bed of trailing ones. Here some exceedingly fine-leaved Achimenes-like plant with modest flowers, and there gorgeous Begonias or some bright-colored Æchmea or Tilland-sia. After planting, this varied collection should be well looked after ; the watering must be carefully done and the plants should be sprayed daily except the ferns. The projecting rocks must be kept constantly moist and the temperature as equable as possible, and varying as little on any side of sixty-five to seventy degrees as practicable. The terrarium should be placed close to a light window, where in case of a strong sunshine it can be shaded, and proper ventilating must never be forgotten. A terrarium constructed somewhat in this way would not be likely to give much trouble, but a vast amount of pleasure and instruction could be had by watching the daily growth of the flora of this miniature world.

Among the numerous plants for this purpose, the following selection will be found suitable : *Dracenas :* Any neat and compact variety. *Palms :* Cocos Weddeliana, Geonoma gracilis. *Aroids :* Curmeria Wallisii, Anthurium, Alocacia, Philodendron, Caladium Argyrites. *Bromeliads :* Small compact varieties. *Ferns :* Pteris serrulata cristata, Adiantum, Lygodium, Trichomanes and Hymenophyllum in deep shade. *Orchids :* Cypripedium. *Clubmosses :* Selaginella Emeliana, S. denticulata, S. apus, S. cæsia, S. viticulosa, S. caulescens, etc. *Miscellaneous Plants :* Eranthemum igneum. Ruellia, Oxalis, Begonia, Peperomia, Pellionia, Fittonia, Maranta, Bertelonia.

X

FRAMES AND PITS

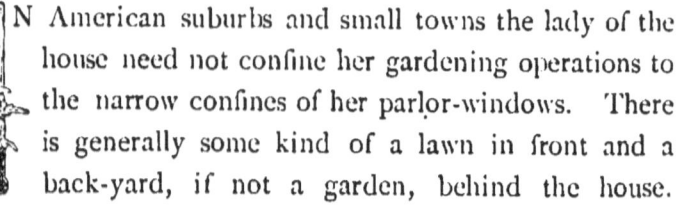N American suburbs and small towns the lady of the house need not confine her gardening operations to the narrow confines of her parlor-windows. There is generally some kind of a lawn in front and a back-yard, if not a garden, behind the house. Where there is ample room for a small pit or green-house it ought to be provided, if special interest is taken in ornamental plants, or where the means will not allow of this a few frames may be very useful. In a pit or greenhouse, which can be heated by means of the same apparatus as the house, many plants can be kept during their growing period, to be brought into the house for decoration when in flower. Here also hardy plants can be forced into flower, sick ones be left to recover, and here also the propagation of plants for the embellishment of the lawn and the borders can be attended to early in the spring, so that they may be ready for immediate use. Potting, tying, cleaning, all can be done here. A greenhouse or pit for general use should be kept at a temperature of from 50 to 60 degrees so as to suit all conditions of plants. The summer temperature would of course, from natural causes, be much higher. The house ought to be provided with canvas-shading and ample means of ventilation.

Frames are useful for storing potted plants for forcing until wanted, and for raising young seedlings in the spring, or for re-pricking seedlings already raised in pots in the window or the greenhouse. If used in spring before frost is over they must be sufficiently covered to exclude too low a temperature, not to mention frost.

XI

LIGHT

IGHT is necessary to all life; the plant cannot develop without its agency. The coloring matter of leaves and flowers is formed under the direct influence of the sun. Different plants require different degrees of light; some rejoice in the full blaze of the sun, others seek the shady retreats of woods and rocks.

Under artificial treatment plants always turn toward the light when it comes from one side only; hence it becomes necessary to turn such plants around frequently to form attractive and regular specimens.

In most dwelling-houses the light, although sufficient, comes from one side only. In summer shade should be provided for many plants against the direct rays of the sun.

While light is beneficial and necessary to the organism of the plant, an excess of light may be injurious and even fatal to its development. Clubmosses, Marantas, and many Ferns will soon succumb in the direct sunlight. Several Palms do best in partial shade. Plants with brightly colored flowers, such as Compositeæ and most succulent plants, enjoy the most ardent sunshine.

XII

TEMPERATURE AND MOISTURE

I N an ordinary dwelling-house a temperature comfortable to live in, viz., of about sixty-five to seventy degrees during the winter months, will also suffice for all plants, even tropical ones. Even Palms in the Southern States stand as low a temperature, at times, as twenty-five degrees without injury. The warm sunshine and the excessive summer heat amply compensate for a rather low winter temperature. The difficulty in America is to raise plants that do well and flower in a rather low temperature, such as the Fuchsias of the high Andes and many beautiful mountain plants from tropical countries. These, as a rule, require plenty of light, but cannot stand excessive heat, and it is only during winter that they can be grown with ease. It is obvious that the range of temperature in a dwelling-house must be rather limited, but some degree of difference can certainly be had. A well-appointed kitchen, when light, will afford a good place for all plants requiring much heat. Next come parlor, library, hall, and other rooms; some of the upper rooms are generally kept at a considerably lower temperature, and an enthusiastic lady who takes interest in window-gardening will certainly avail herself of these for many plants barely needing protection from frost. Cool cellars can be used for storing hardy plants destined to be forced during the winter.

In many dwelling-houses the atmosphere is excessively dry, and where this is the case a good many useful plants cannot be grown.   Many kinds of insects are liable to attack plants in a dry atmosphere.   Much can be done to overcome this trouble by spraying the foliage often, or by growing plants that require a great deal of moisture in terrariums or double windows. Many Ferns, Orchids, and tropical foliage-plants require an atmosphere laden with moisture.   Cacti, many kinds of bulbous plants, Palms, and Bromeliads, as also many florist-flowers, do well in a dry room, but all except Cacti need occasional washings and sprayings.

A room in which the atmosphere is kept sweet and buoyant by means of heating and ventilation, can produce as good flowers as the best greenhouse.

XIII

INSECTS AND DISEASES

GREENFLIES are the most formidable of the insect foes we have to deal with on house-plants. They come on the young growing shoots of most plants, and if left alone increase with marvellous rapidity. In greenhouses they can easily be dealt with, as one or two good strong smokings with tobacco-stalks will destroy all fully developed insects. In a house where fumigation is out of the question greenflies must be got rid of by means of washing, dipping in weak tobacco water, or by dusting the young shoots with tobacco powder. Mealy-bug is a curious, disagreeable insect, and cannot be got rid of except by washing it away with a sponge or picking it out of the axis of leaves and other corners where it cannot be otherwise reached. It does not, however, increase in any alarming degree, and with a little ordinary care is not likely to cause any trouble in a house. The same can be said of the scales, a similar kind of insect that is frequently found on American trees such as the Sassafras and the Chionanthus.

The Thrips and the Red Spider are liable to attack many plants if kept too dry. The only means of freeing house-plants of these is by a good, thorough washing with a strong solution of fir-tree oil or some other insecticide ; they can generally be kept away by keeping the foliage sufficiently moist. In this case prevention is decidedly better than cure.

Earth-worms when in pots can easily be removed by the hand ; their presence is indicated by the small globular masses of excrement that they deposit on the surface of the soil.

Slugs, if accidentally brought into the house, may cause considerable damage on tender growing shoots, and should be watched for after bringing plants from the outside. Mice, if not prevented, will sometimes disturb young seeds. A good remedy is to cover all seed-pots with a flat piece of glass.

Diseases may arise from injudicious watering, subjections to droughts, previous attacks of insects, or through insufficient drainage. Mildew is caused by sudden chills; it attacks young, growing foliage and shoots. It can be effectually stopped by dusting the affected parts with flower of sulphur. Many forms of fungi attack greenhouse plants, but are not much to be afraid of in the case of a few well-looked after house-plants.

When the leaves of any plant turn sickly yellow, something is generally the matter with the root, and it should immediately be turned out and carefully examined. If the cause is not apparent a removal of the old soil, and in some cases a thorough cleaning of the root, re-potting in fresh and suitable soil, and very careful watering until new roots are formed, will effect a cure. If the sickness is caused by bad drainage the remedy is evident. Strong sunshine will sometimes scorch the leaves. This of course is not a disease, but disfigures the plant all the same. To prevent this, shade all tender-leaved plants.

XIV

DECORATION

oliage and other plants. Having been successful in raising and growing to perfection a number of decorative plants, the grower naturally desires to arrange them in the most satisfactory and effective manner, and a few hints to this effect will perhaps not be out of place. If the apartments are large, light, and airy, a more satisfactory result can be obtained than in small and dull rooms, for many plants can in that case be disposed in some of the inner corners of the apartment. Indeed many Palms and other foliage-plants do not object to a little shade.

To begin in the hall ; the foot of the staircase is admirable for displaying large foliage-plants of the Dracena type or Palms. A strong, beautiful specimen of either, or a small group on either side with a tall, pinnately leaved Palm in the centre edged with smaller Palms, Caladiums, Silk-oaks, Sanchesias, or even some suitable plants in flowers, where the hall is large. A specimen on either side of the entrance, of sufficient size to cause a beautiful display, or some climbing plants covering the wainscoting of the door and rising in garlands to the ceiling, is simple and effective. In the parlor a somewhat more luxurious display can be allowed. Oleanders in bloom, specimens of India-rubber trees, Aurucarias, simple but effective specimens of some Palm, can be placed in nooks and corners. On spacious mantel-pieces a fine specimen of some flowering plant at each side is not out of place. On either side of windows, or on the window-sill, tastefully arranged flowering plants may be allowed. The central table may be decorated with a single specimen of some graceful Palm proportionate in size. In the

Bracket with Plant of *Saxifraga sarmentosa.*

dining-room suitable plants may be arranged on cupboards, mantel-piece, on either side of the window, and on the table.

Special single stands and brackets can of course be provided for many plants in any room. Brackets are especially useful for climbing and trailing plants.

In the kitchen, of course, the plants need not be at all conventionally arranged, the desire being simply to give a cheerful, home-like aspect to the place. This indeed may be said about all arrangement of plants where comfort and pleasure are more studied than gorgeous effect and conventional display. Simplicity should be the first law in all things connected with floral decoration. Any overcrowding, any plants placed so as to obstruct views of pictures or to hide furniture, or so as to make it difficult to move about, are decidedly out of place.

Cut flowers in vases are often desirable in bed-rooms, in the library, and on the table, and most American woods and fields offer a host of beautiful plants for this purpose. In spring the May flowers, the blue Anemone, the Meadow Beauty, the numerous Phloxes, beautiful Orchids, Azaleas, Mountain Laurel, and numerous others offer rich treasures for home adornment. In summer we have Rudbeckias, later on Golden Rods, Asters, and a variety of autumn leaves in brilliant colors. Cut flowers, to keep fresh as long as possible, should be kept constantly in fresh water. Some of the frailest of flowers will often keep beautiful longer than larger ones. The common Forget-me-not, if gathered in bud and made into wreaths, and placed in water on a common dinner-plate, will grow and flower for a long period, making a perfect mass of blue.

Jardinières, china pots, and pots of earthenware in ornamental designs can be employed for placing round the pots in which plants are grown, if these are not considered sufficiently ornamental in themselves.

Jardinières, besides being ornamental, are very useful for protecting the roots of tender plants from over-exposure to sunshine and drought.

Pots protected by these or other suitable vessels will always keep sufficiently cool.

XV

BASKETS, VASES, AND WINDOW BOXES

MANY trailing plants and vines are well suited for growing in hanging baskets, vases, and window boxes. Baskets can be made either of earthenware or china, or of pieces of wood, or iron or copper wire. Baskets of the latter type must be clothed with moss to keep the soil in position, and by reason of the excellent drainage are eminently suited to Ferns and Orchids. "Baskets" of china or earthenware are rather more ornamental and better fitted to plants of more solid growth, such as Ivy-leaved Geraniums, Ivy, and even small Palms and Dracenas. In planting baskets care should be taken to make the bottom solid, so as not to risk the falling out of the soil afterward when least expected.

Vases are suitable ornaments for stoops and entrances to a house. Filled with Palms, large Century-plants, or Dracenas, they make a beautiful effect. Even in the house, on the newels of staircases or on single stands, vases with suitable plants are very ornamental. Large cast-iron vases, such as are usually used in cemeteries and gardens, can be made very attractive by planting with a variety of plants. One way is to plant a large Palm or Dracena in the centre and fill out with various foliage and flowering plants, such as Begonias, Marguerites, Ivy, and Coleus; and for edging, Verbenas, Lobelias, and various kinds

of Mesembryanthemums.   There should be no crowding, however, but each species should have ample room for development.

Window-boxes are largely used in England, and when well
planted are exceedingly beautiful.   They are made of wood,

Window-Box.

about eight inches wide and deep, by a length to fit the width
of the window, and are placed outside the window on the projecting sill.   Where this does not project sufficiently, iron

brackets can be placed just below the window, and will be just as safe. The bottom, or better, the whole inside, can be covered with zinc perforated in the bottom to allow for drainage. Begonias, tuberous and herbaceous, Calceolarias, Fuchsias, and choice Geraniums are favorite flowers for this purpose. The boxes are often edged with Lobelia, Musk, Alternanthera, and other low-growing plants. Marguerites, Heliotropes, Verbenas, and Dracenas may also be used with advantage. Ivies and creeping vines are largely employed in window-boxes; hanging down in graceful garlands or partially trained round the window, they make a very charming effect.

Flower-stands of cast iron in ornamental designs are very useful for growing a large number of plants in a small space. The tops should be flat, with a shallow tray of zinc for holding the plants. The illustration printed herewith shows a suitable stand nicely arranged. The central plant is a small and graceful Palm, and around this are placed a number of foliage and flowering plants.

The best plants for growing in hanging baskets and window-boxes are as centre plants: Anthericum variegatum, Dracena indivisa, Abutilon, Bromelia Ananas variegata, Geranium, Heliotrope, Paris Daisy, Pandanus, Solanum jasminoides. For border around these the following may be used: Begonia semperflorens and varieties, B. metallica, B. fuchsioides, Ivy-leaved Geraniums, German Ivy, Ivy, Cuphea, Libonia, Coleus, Irisine. For edging the following varieties are very suitable: Alyssum, Musk, Periwinkle, Verbena, Lobelia, variegated forms of Tropæolum; Manettia, Tradescantia, and others according to circumstances. Vases may be filled with similar plants, or with large single specimens of American Aloe, Dracena indivisa, and others according to size.

Plant Stand.

XVI

THE VERANDA, AND HOW TO ADORN IT

N the summer-time many of the floral treasures of the house can be profitably employed to decorate the veranda. Large Palms can be placed at regular intervals. Passion flowers and other vines can be trained to pillars and trellis-work, and hanging baskets may be suspended from the ceiling between the columns. Even outside the windows or bordering the main entrance, trellises can be placed for flowering vines, of which there are very many suitable species.

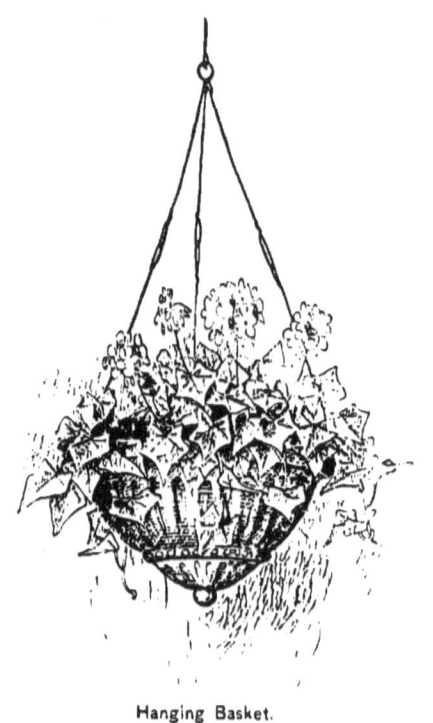

Hanging Basket.

Between the pillars continuous boxes with rich displays of foliage and flowers may be had, and beautiful vases on the stoops and near the approach to the steps. All this floral luxury need not involve any heavy outlay of money, but a great deal of forethought is of course necessary to have everything ready in due time.

We beg our women readers to carefully study the descriptions of suitable plants in the following part. There, every advice necessary to insure success will be given, and by careful study of the directions therein, the reader will no doubt be able to make her home as attractive as plants and flowers can make it.

PART II

THE SELECTION OF HOUSE PLANTS

I

ON PLANT NAMES

ANY exotic plants have no authorized American names, and their Latin names being in most instances simple and euphonious, should be used in preference to any doubtful American name. Many plants are given different whimsical names in different States, and the practice of dispensing with a good Latin name such as Begonia, for the very ridiculous "angel's wings," as I heard it called in one instance, can only lead to the most deplorable confusion. The floral world is so rich, its different species are of such peculiar relation to each other, that it would be simply impossible to invent common names for all. Such beautiful Latin names as Camellia, Azalea, Reseda, Viola, Citrus, Mimosa and others, are superior to most common names in brevity and simplicity. Many ignorant florists, as I know from experience, invent names to suit customers and circumstances, but such liberties are as inexcusable as they are dishonest.

In the descriptions of plants I shall in all cases give the American names that exist and are universally recognized. In all other cases the Latin names alone are given.

Many plants, especially varieties raised by florists, have however only names given to distinguish them from other varieties of the same species, such as all double flowers of

Roses, Chrysanthemums, Carnations, Geraniums, and other plants.

A word of warning may here be given against anything unusually marvellous in the world of horticulture—things that never have existed and never will. The floral world, indeed, contains sufficiently marvellous things, gorgeous works of the Creator that need no gilding and no improvement.

II

ROSES, CARNATIONS, AND CHRYSANTHEMUMS

EVERAL varieties of the Rose are admirably adapted for window culture, and when of a bushy habit, with strong and glossy foliage, and producing fine flowers, there are no prettier plants than these. Roses require plenty of fresh air, sunshine, and a steady temperature; as also a constant moisture at the root. The foliage, to keep fresh and free from insects, needs frequent sprayings or an occasional immersion in pure water.

The best varieties for our purpose are some of the smaller, rich-flowering Tea roses, such as Niphitos, a white and very beautiful rose with long pointed buds; Perle des jardins, with globular yellow flowers; La France, a well-known erect variety with silvery-pink flowers; Catherine Mermet, pink, and the Bride, a pure white form. Clotilde Soupert is a small pink rose of great beauty and a profuse bloomer; it is the very best variety for window culture. The Fairy roses are perhaps equally suitable. They are miniature roses producing clusters of flowers in great profusion and forming very dwarf and compact plants. The rosy-pink Burgundy and its white variety are the best.

To propagate the Rose, select wood from a shoot that has just finished flowering, take the part immediately below the flower, and make cuttings with two or three buds, leaving the top leaf.

Cut obliquely immediately below a bud and remove the marrow from the lower end.   Prepare a well-drained pot, fill it partly with sharp silver-sand which should be pressed down very firmly.   Insert the cuttings one by one nearly down to the leaf.   The outer ones may very well touch the inside of the pot.   Then water well and keep constantly moist and in a light position in about 60 degrees, where, in the course of three or four weeks, they will all be rooted.   Then remove from the sand, pot singly in 2-inch pots, very firmly and without injuring the roots.   Re-pot as often as necessary until established in 7- or 8-inch pots, in which they should be allowed to bloom. Roses require rich soil: two parts of good fibrous loam, one part decayed cow manure, with a sprinkle of bone-dust and some sand, makes a good soil for flowering plants.   After some time the soil should be top-dressed, and late in the season weak manure water will do good.

To make the plants bushy and strong, all flower-buds appearing during the summer should be removed.   Shoots producing no flower-buds should be trimmed back to about two strong buds in September or October.   During the winter months the plants will bloom freely if properly cared for.   All shoots after flowering should be cut back to a good bud.

Look well after watering in summer, spray foliage frequently, allow no green-flies or mildew to get a foothold on any account.

Carnations, next to the rose, have been favorites with florists for centuries.   The Carnation is a plant well fitted for house culture, neat in habit, easily grown and very floriferous ; there is no better plant to be had.   Of American varieties the white Silver-spray, the yellow Buttercup, the salmon-pink Daybreak, the rose-pink Tidal-wave and the scarlet Portia are among the best.

Carnations should be propagated during the winter or spring months. Cuttings made of growing side-shoots are the best; the lower leaves are simply removed and the tips shortened. It is also good practice to split the lower end, inducing it to root from a larger surface. As soon as rooted, pot in 2-inch pots pretty firmly in light sandy soil. Re-pot two or three times, plant out in border for summer months, nip long-growing shoots and buds, and pot in about September in 5- or 6-inch pots. If there is no garden, the little plants can very well be grown on in the house in pots, but should have plenty of air and light.

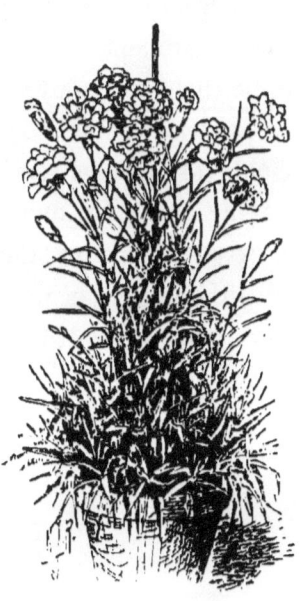

Carnation.
Dianthus caryophyllus plenus.

Soil made up of three parts loam, one part sand, and one part decayed manure will suit all carnations. During the winter months they should be kept in a cooler room than roses, if possible, and have plenty of light.

Chrysanthemums are becoming more and more popular, especially the large flowering Japanese kinds. The incurved Chinese varieties are, however, better suited for home culture, as they produce more flowers.

Good lists of varieties are found in all catalogues and can be obtained of all florists.

To propagate, keep plants after flowering in a cool place, remove the old stems, and as soon as the young shoots appear at the base and are about three inches long, make the cuttings.

Simply remove the lower leaves, cut the end with a sharp knife, and shorten the foliage slightly. Insert in sand as recommended for Roses and Carnations. Water well and keep in a light place in about 45 degrees until rooted. Pot and treat as Carnations. The soil must be rich, that recommended for Roses will do very well. Chrysanthemums, however, should be potted less firmly. In July the plants should be potted in 8- or 10-inch pots, if sufficiently large, and should then be plunged outside or kept where the pot can remain shaded at all times while the plant enjoys plenty of light.

As soon as the young buds appear, the superfluous ones should at once be removed from the axis of the lower leaves, leaving only from one to six on the same shoot, according to variety. Now also stimulating liquid manure should be given until the flowers begin to expand, when water should be given more sparingly. If kept cool and dry the flowers keep longest.

III

POPULAR FLORIST FLOWERS

Balsams are well-known annuals. There are many strains of seeds, some giving more, others less double flowers, the double-flowered ones only being of any value. The colors of Balsams are extremely tender and beautiful, varying from white to deep-red, either one-colored or mottled or striped. Camellia flowered Balsams are the largest and finest.

Balsams should be sown in March or April, or even later, for late bloom in the house. Place a few seeds in 2-inch pots, and when rooting through the soil re-pot into larger ones repeatedly until the plants are in 5- or 6-inch pots, in which they may flower. The young seedlings should be kept in the warmest and lightest apartment. Turn the plants round frequently, as they grow toward the light. Two parts of loam, one of well-decayed leaf mould and horse manure, and one of sand makes a good soil.

Begonias. Begonias are among the most beautiful and easiest grown house plants. Of late years there have been raised a number of hybrids and varieties excelling in beauty of form and color any known species. Begonias grown for their flowers are of two kinds. One group with tuberous roots, the other shrubby. *Tuberous rooted* Begonias are raised from seeds which are extremely fine, and must be sown on the surface of the soil in a pot covered with a flat piece of glass and kept moist, shaded, and in a temperature of about 60 or 65 degrees. When the extremely small seedlings are sufficiently large to be handled they should be pricked out in pans or pots, later on singly in small pots. The best kinds are :

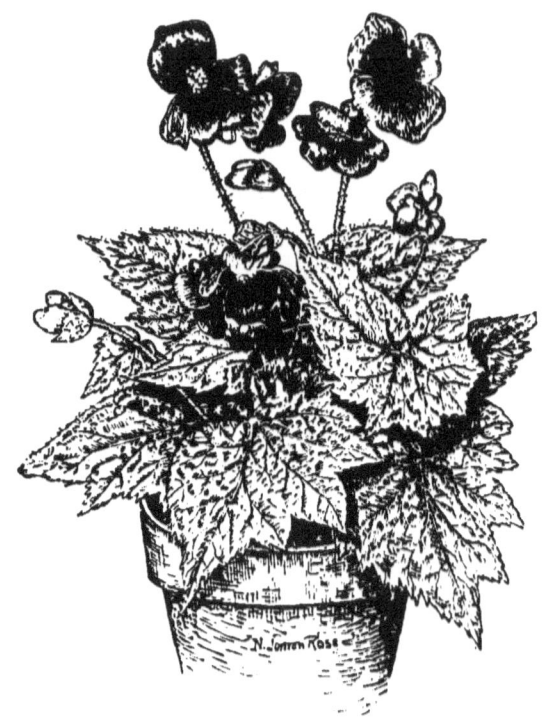

Tuberous-rooted Begonia.

B. boliviensis. Leaves three to four inches, triangular, serrate. Flowers in large drooping clusters, scarlet, summer-flowering.

B. Davisii. Low, compact ; leaves rounded, heart-shaped, green on upper surface, red below, hairy. Inflorescence four to five inches high, flowers red, in umbellate clusters. Very beautiful.

B. Frœbelii.   Stemless, leaves heart-shaped, with long point ; green, somewhat hairy.   Flowers large, scarlet, in loose, drooping clusters on tall stems ; winter-flowering.   Very fine.

B. Pearceii.   Succulent bushy stem.   Leaves narrowly cordate, pointed, toothed ; smooth above, hairy and red below. Flowers large, yellow from the axils of the leaves, in large clusters.   Beautiful.   Summer.

B. rosæflora.   Compact, stemless.   Leaves rather large, hairy below, rounded in outline, edge reddish, toothed.   Flowers very large on strong woolly stems, rosy-red.   Summer.

There are many beautiful varieties and hybrids.   Ordinary seed packets of tuberous-rooted Begonias contain many of the best varieties, but generally not the above species, which must be bought separately.   Most of the varieties are good for outdoor bedding as well as for the house.

Shrubby Begonias are generally propagated by cuttings. They root easily but are inclined to rot if kept too damp or too cold.   Bottom heat of about 70 degrees is preferable but not necessary when the main temperature is about or above that.   These can also be propagated by seeds, but more slowly.

Good kinds are the following species and varieties :

B. Bruantii.   Bushy.   Flowers white, tinted rose, in rich upright clusters.   Leaves brownish-green.

B. coccinea.   Shrubby, one to two feet.   Leaves long and pointed.   Flowers in drooping clusters from the axils of the leaves, red scarlet.   One of the best.

B. corallina.   Tall-growing, shrubby species.   Flowers in loose axillar clusters, large, winged, coral-red.

B. fuchsioides.   Bushy, erect.   Small leaves and flowers in loose drooping racemes, somewhat fuchsia-like, scarlet.   Summer-flowering.

B. maculata. Leaves deep dull green, spotted with white on the upper side, smooth, reddish below. Flowers in small clusters, coral-red, varying to white.

B. manicata. Large, luxurious foliage, compact habit. Leaves glossy, dark green, obliquely cordate, pointed. Flowers small, numerous, in erect clusters above the foliage, pink or fleshy. Ornamental. Variety, with white, maculated foliage, common.

Begonia semperflorens rosea gigantea.

B. semperflorens (Ice-plant), most common species. Leaves fleshy, glossy. Flowers numerous, medium size, white.

Varieties rosea and rosea gigantia, extremely beautiful tall-growing varieties, with large shining leaves and immense axillary clusters of very large rosy flowers. Best Begonia grown, ever-blooming.

B. Weltoniensis. Very common species of a bushy habit, with small green leaves tinted crimson, and numerous small flowers of a pale rose. Very valuable as a house plant.

Newer varieties: Erfordiæ, very good. Gloire de Sceaux, Gloire de Lorraine, and others.

For Begonias with ornamental leaves see Miscellaneous Foliage-plants.

Soil for Begonias should be light and fibrous, of equal parts fibrous loam and leaf mould and a liberal addition of sharp sand. Pots must be well drained.

Calceolarias are of two kinds, herbaceous and shrubby.

Calceolaria hybrida is the common large flowered kind, grown in greenhouses, and remarkable for their curiously, often brilliantly colored flowers of a mottled, speckled, or one-colored tint.

These are raised from seeds sown in summer on the surface of the soil in well-drained pots, as recommended for Begonias. Must be kept moist until growing by means of shading. Keep the seed-pots in a rather cool place, re-prick as usual, gradually in single pots, and re-pot until in 6-inch pots, in which the plants can be wintered in a cool, light place. They bloom in summer and need careful watering, and must be kept free from greenflies. Soil as for Begonias, with the addition of a little well-rotted manure.

Cineraria, cruenta variety.

The shrubby Calceolarias are mostly used for out-door bedding, but are rather pretty in pots. They grow taller, more bushy, and are more floriferous than the herbaceous kinds, but less varied in color, which is mostly yellow or brown.

Cinerarias are pretty annuals of a very varied range of vivid coloring. There are double varieties, which are less desirable; dwarf kinds, and ordinary ones. Sow in April or May to obtain winter-blooming plants, in light sandy soil, cover lightly, keep moist and partially shaded until sprouting. Cover seed-pots with glass. When large enough, prick out singly in 2-inch pots, grow on, and re-pot frequently. Must be kept during summer as cool as possible, and are benefited by frequent sprayings. Keep off insects! Pot in rich, fibrous soil, water plentifully every day—twice if necessary.

Chinese Primulas are very neat winter-blooming plants, raised from seeds or, in the case of some double varieties, by cuttings. Either method is easy. There are numerous varieties from white to lilac. Sow in pots or shallow pans successively from March to July, cover lightly, keep moist and partially shaded until growing, leave the plants for some time in seed-pots. Plant singly in 2-inch pots; when large enough keep on re-potting as soon as well rooted. Soil rich fibrous, same as recommended for Cinerarias.

Chinese Primula. *Primula sinensis.*

Flower in 4- or 5-inch pots. A cold frame where available is best for the summer, for this as well as for Cinerarias, Cyclamens, Calceolarias, and Marguerites.

Cyclamens. Persian Alp-violet. Beautiful plants of the *Primula* family in a variety of colors. Buy corms or propagate by seeds. Sow fresh seeds in September in pots well drained and filled with light sandy soil, cover about a quarter of an inch, and put a light covering of chopped moss on the surface, if on hand. Keep in about 60 degrees until sprouting, leave until large enough to be potted in 2-inch pots. . Re-pot once or twice during the winter, leaving the little corms just in the surface of the soil. Keep in a cool shady place in summer, and spray leaves frequently in warm weather. In about fifteen months the young plants should flower, and the strongest will then be in 6-inch pots. Young home-grown plants are the best.

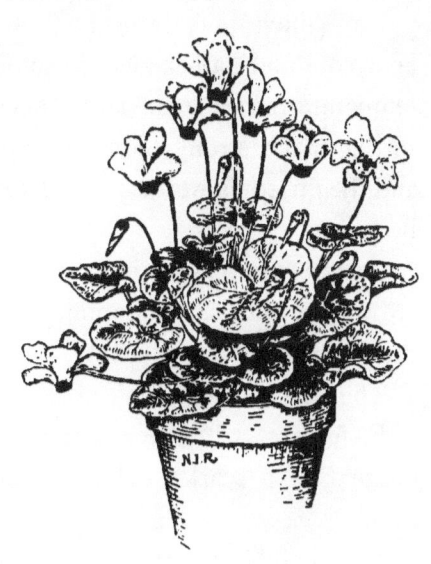

Persian Violet. *Cyclamen persicum.*

Corms bought and grown on are not as floriferous, and often fail. The plants may be rested after flowering, and grown a second year with success. Rich leaf mould and fibrous loam with sand and a little well-decayed manure make a good soil. The plants require plenty of water while growing. These are extremely elegant and attractive plants when covered with flowers; they flower during a long part of the winter.

Fuchsias, owing to climatic conditions, cannot be grown as well here as in Europe, where they are seen in every cottage-window. Still a moderate success may be obtained, especially in the Northern States and in mountain districts. There is an enormous number of species and varieties, all of which are easily propagated by means of half-ripe cuttings. Root these in a pot filled with sharp sand, kept light and moist. The cuttings root quickly in spring, and can soon be potted in 3- or 4-inch pots in light but rich soil. They should be kept cool and half-shaded in summer, and the ordinary winter temperature of a room suits them well. Plants raised in the spring make strong flowering specimens by the next spring, and begin to flower early. During winter a slight rest may be given.

Some of the species have small but very elegant flowers and are very floriferous, and none of the gorgeous double varieties can vie with them in beauty.

The best species are:

F. fulgens, with very long trumpet-like flowers in drooping clusters of a scarlet color. Leaves heart-shaped, large and robust.

F. gracilis is a very elegant and rich-blooming species, with axillary small purplish flowers.

F. splendens, with green and scarlet flowers. Very early flowering and beautiful.

F. globosa is a common, beautiful species.

Of the numerous varieties a good selection is kept in most greenhouses.

Geraniums, or Zonal Pelargoniums, are great favorites, because of their easy culture and dazzling colors. The new Bruant varieties and some of the old double kinds are the best for house culture. Geraniums are easily raised by means of cuttings at any time of the year. They root easily and can be immediately put in 3-inch pots and re-potted as soon as well rooted. Soil, rich and light—not particular.

The best varieties are all found in florists' catalogues.

For Ivy-leaved Geraniums see Trailers.

Stocks and Wallflowers are very neat and easily grown subjects. Stocks for winter-flowering should be sown in summer, pricked off into separate pots when sufficiently large, and grown on as rapidly as possible until in 6-inch pots. They should be nipped frequently to make them bushy, and must have a cool and light place with plenty of water during the summer. Seeds produce only a certain percentage of double flowers. These varieties, if exceptionally fine, can, although the plant is considered annual, be readily propagated by means of cuttings, simply made of short growing side-shoots. The Wallflower is perennial, half-woody, and produces extremely fragrant single or double flowers, varying in colors from light yellow to deep brown. Unlike the single Stocks, single Wallflowers are valuable and elegant. They are raised in the same way as Stocks but are better increased by cuttings. Soil for Stocks and Wallflowers must be rich, porous, and should contain a certain portion of old mortar if obtainable. Wallflowers are so called because they often grow on old brick walls and ruins, where there is no apparent moisture or nutriment, but where they develop none the less well.

Gloxinias are tuberous-rooted plants, with thick fleshy leaves and large and showy bell-shaped flowers. They are very rich in coloration, one-colored, dotted or blotched on either dark or light bottom. The tubers can easily be obtained, but it is better to buy the plants in bud or raise them from seeds. Seeds are fine and should be treated in every particular like those of tuberous-rooted Begonias. They should, however, be sown earlier and kept somewhat warmer. The treatment is otherwise similar. The plants flower early in spring and summer, and should be kept cool and shaded while in flower. Gloxinias are also readily increased by means of leaf-cuttings. If tubers are bought, they should be started in a warm place about mid-winter or earlier. Gentle sprayings are beneficial, and a half-shaded position suits them best.

Gloxinia.

Heliotropes are favorite flowers and, as they are easily grown, should be in all collections. They require a warm tempera-ture and plenty of moisture. They are increased by means of herbaceous, brittle cuttings inserted in sand close to the rim of a pot and kept warm. The cuttings should be allowed to root well before being potted separately. To make bushy, sturdy plants, pinch the young shoots often and keep the plants in a light place. Ordinary light and rich soil.

The Marguerite or Paris daisy is a kind of single Chrysan-themum. It flowers from the earliest spring throughout sum-mer, and is especially valuable because it can be had in flower early in the season. There are several white and yellow varieties, the white ones being most valuable. Increased by means of cuttings taken any time of the year, if brittle and herbaceous. Soil as for Geraniums and treatment similar.

Pelargonium. Show- or English Pelargoniums are increased in and grown in the same way as Geraniums, but in somewhat richer and more solid soil. Some of the varieties are extremely beautiful, of vivid, velvety colors. They flower during spring and summer and bloom for a long time, but not continuously as Geraniums. The Martha Washington variety is most common in America. Others can be had of most florists.

The Petunias. Double Petunias are raised from cuttings, and after rooting and the first potting do well under a treatment and in soil similar to that for Geraniums. Petunias are somewhat difficult to root, and they must be prevented from rotting. The cuttings should be made of soft and brittle wood and split in the lower end. They should be potted rather firmly and kept shaded for a day or two afterward. There are many richly colored, striped, and mottled varieties, as also unicolored ones. White varieties are the best.

IV

CACTI

THE Cactus family is one of the most curious plant families that exist. It is generally characterized by monstrous, fleshy, leafless and prickly stems, sometimes covered with hairs and wool. There are many species, with exceedingly large, beautiful flowers, that flower in a night and must be watched for, to be seen. Most species of the handsomest genus in the order, the Phyllocactus, flower, however, for a considerable period and are then beautiful beyond comparison. Cacti are found in hot and dry countries on barren hillsides, where for years they exist and develop without any visible supply of water. They can hardly be killed by drought, but careless watering must be avoided. Moderate watering during the growing season is all that is needed. The soil should be gravelly and light, and a special good drainage must always be provided for. These plants enjoy all the sunshine that can be had, but will do well in a not too heavy shade.

Cereus is a very extensive genus of mostly erect, columnar, hairy, and spiny plants. There are, however, some climbing and trailing plants belonging to this genus of great beauty. It is chiefly these that are of any value for our purpose. C. flagelliformis is a little plant with finger-thick, cylindrical, hairy and spiny stems, and an abundance of pink flowers in the spring. It can be grown in small hanging baskets of earthenware.

C. grandiflorus. This is a night-blooming species with large gorgeous flowers of a whitish yellow like a big star. Very fragrant. Flowers in the summer.

C. Mallisonii is one of the most beautiful of all cacti. It has long slender stems, and is one of the most profuse bloomers. The flowers are of medium size, of a bright scarlet-crimson color. The plant will continue to flower for a considerable period.

C. speciosissimus is a very showy plant, with soft and slender three to four angled stems and whitish aërial roots. Blooms profusely in the summer. Flowers medium-sized, rosy-scarlet.

Epiphyllum truncatum is a little, rich-flowering species with drooping two-winged stems. It is generally grafted on some other cactus to bring it above the ground. Flowers generally rose-purple, with many varieties, expand in winter or spring. When not grafted it is suitable for hanging baskets.

Echinocactus and **Echinopsis** are short and globular forms with many varieties. They are ribbed and hairy, and sometimes covered with formidable spines. Flowers generally very fine.

Melocactus and **Mammillaria,** the one globular and ribbed, the other generally consisting of fleshy, pap-like protuberances, hairy and spiny, very elegant and ornamental. Flower rarely, and although beautiful, of less importance on that account.

Opuntia (Indian Fig). Is a common genus all over the Southern States. Some species have large and showy yellow flowers; others are more remarkable on account of their curious growth. Some Opuntias are tall and robust plants, with flat-jointed or cylindrical stems.   As they are easily grown and rather picturesque, they may be worth a trial.

Pereskia is a plant with rich and luxuriant foliage, and although spiny, greatly different in appearance from most other Cacti.   It is of a rambling habit, and as it is hardy in the south, is generally used to cover verandas and porches.   The flowers, though pretty, are insignificant.

Phyllocactus Ackermannii.

Phyllocactus deserves universal culture, not only for its flowers but because of its neat, ornamental habit.   There are several species, of which some are night-flowering.

P. Ackermannii has beautiful crimson flowers on slender flattened stems of a fine green color. It has a rather bushy habit, and when covered with flowers in the summer is very handsome.

P. crenatus, with creamy-white flowers, has many varieties ; scarlet, orange, pink, and crimson. This is one of the finest and most widely grown species.

P. phyllanthoides is a very floriferous form, with pale rose-colored flowers on flattened crenated stems.

Phyllocactus, several Cereus, Opuntias, and Pereskias can easily be increased by means of cuttings, which, after taking, should be allowed to lie a day or two before inserted.   Any piece of the stem provided with a bud will generally grow, but young, just ripened shoots are the best.   The globular-shaped forms of Cacti enumerated above are increased by seed ; but this being a slow process, they should be bought from a collection, as they are inexpensive. Phyllocactus, Cereus, Opuntia, and Pereskia should be grown in rich, sandy soil.

V

OTHER SUCCULENTS

HERE are numerous succulent plants of an extremely neat habit, with bright-colored, attractive flowers, such as Sempervivums, Crassulas, and Echeverias that, although inferior in size, are very ornamental in a window. The following are a few of the most interesting kinds:

Cotyledon. Navelwort. This is a genus of plants with fleshy, wedge-shaped leaves disposed in rosettes, neat and compact in habit, which reproduce themselves freely by means of offsets. Most of the species are hardy. The genus includes *Echeveria*, of which E. agavoides, coccinea, metallica, Peacockii, and secunda are well-known plants used in carpet-bedding. They produce racemes of charming, mostly orange or orange-scarlet or red flowers. These plants are useful in window-boxes, or for bordering large vases.

Crassula jasminea.

Crassula and **Rochea** are nearly allied plants. C. coccinea is a plant of an erect habit, about a foot high, with slender stems and small triangular, fleshy leaves, bearing a head of long tubular scarlet flowers in winter or spring. C. jasminea is similar to this in habit, but has white flowers. Propagated by cuttings that should lie a day or two before insertion. A light, rich, sandy soil is suitable. Well-grown plants of these are very ornamental and last a long time in flower.

Rochea falcata is one of the oldest inhabitants in gardens. It is a curious-looking plant, with 2 to 3 inches long falcate, thick and fleshy leaves, disposed spirally on the rather tall stems. Has nice crimson flowers, and is very picturesque at all times. Soil as above, with addition of old mortar or similar stuff.

Bryophyllum is a tall-growing shrub, with long pinnately divided fleshy leaves, remarkable for the quality of forming numerous little plants at the termination of the veins on the notched edge. It is thus easily propagated. The flowers are insignificant. Soil as for Crassula.

Mesembryanthemums are curious, fleshy, often shrubby plants, with flowers in outward appearance resembling Asters or Daisies. The flowers are generally handsome and brightly colored, and expand in sunshine.

M. australe is a kind sometimes seen in American greenhouses. It has slender, shrubby, creeping stems, and will be seen on bright summer days, completely covered with numerous small, bright-pink flowers. Leaves very small and fleshy. Good for hanging-baskets or window-boxes.

M. caulescens is another pretty, shrubby kind, with long, awl-shaped leaves, and rather large, rose-colored, fragrant flowers.

M. cordifolium variegatum, with variegated leaves and creeping stems, is chiefly remarkable for its foliage. Propagated by seeds or cuttings. This plant is very useful in vases, baskets, and window-boxes, and is largely used for carpet-bedding.

M. multiflorum, with white flowers and some varieties, and M. pomeridianum, with very large yellow flowers, are also common. Ordinary light, sandy soil.

Sedum Sieboldii is a very fine, old house plant, low and trailing in habit, and admirably suited for hanging baskets. Leaves roundish, three in a whorl. Flowers in umbellate cymes, pink. There is a fine variety with variegated leaves.

Sempervivums (House-leek) are plants somewhat similar to Echeverias in habit, having numerous leaves disposed in rosettes. Leaves less fleshy, generally spatulate. S. Arborescens is a rather handsome shrub, with racemes of yellow flowers. S. Arachnoideum is remarkable for its covering of threads like a spider's web. S. tabulæforme has wide, absolutely flat rosettes of leaves, and tall peduncles with numerous yellow flowers.

Aloe belongs to the lily family, and consists of numerous species of tall, gaudy shrubs, with long and grotesque fleshy leaves, smaller but not unlike those of a Century-plant. The leaves are glaucous, or green, or with conspicuous black spots. The flowers are born in erect racemes and are tubular, generally greenish-yellow, with a red apex.

Aloe variegata is one of the most common plants to be seen in windows in Europe. It is very pretty, with spotted leaves.

A. vera, saponaria, cæsia, and other forms are larger, and as young plants are very suitable. Propagated by cuttings or seeds. Soil rich and sandy, with an admixture of old brick rubbish and mortar. Pots to be well drained.

Gasteria is a plant similar in habits to the Aloe, but much smaller. These are neat plants for the window, and very decorative, in or out of bloom. G. maculata, variolosa, and verrucosa are especially beautiful, with tall graceful spikes of flowers.

American Aloe. *Agave americana.*

Agave. American Aloe. The common Century-plant or American Aloe is too well known to need description. Its decorative use is well known, and its culture very easy. There are, however, a few smaller species of the same genus that deserve a trial for the sake of their neat habit. Among these suffice it to mention: A. filifera, with long pointed leaves. A. Roezliana, with a rosette of comparatively short leaves. A. Victoriæ Reginæ and A. Yuccæfolia.

Othonna crassifolia is a curious plant of the composite family, with cylindrical, fleshy leaves of a glaucous color, and small yellow flowers on long, slender petioles. The stems are trailing, almost thread-like. Fine for hanging-baskets. Soil rich and fibrous with plenty of sand, ordinary.

VI

THE LILY AND AMARYLLIS FAMILIES

MANY attractive plants belong to these families, and as they are easily grown, have become quite popular. Some have bulbs, other fleshy roots and rootstocks; they are chiefly propagated by offsets.

Agapanthus umbellatus. African Lily. This is a strong growing, ever-green plant, with long, strap-shaped leaves and tall scapes, with umbells of azure flowers. It requires plenty of moisture and rich soil, and develops rapidly under good treatment to fine specimens. The plants should be allowed to increase in size year after year, as large plants are very handsome when in flower. Large tubs, boxes, or pots will be required for strong specimens.

Amaryllis is a genus of beautiful bulbous plants, with mostly ever-green leaves. During the growing season, from early spring to the fall, the plants require abundant water. After that they should have a slight rest until January or February, but must not be entirely dried off, when they will soon bloom. Good, rich, yet light and somewhat sandy, soil is most suitable.

A. Ackermanni has large crimson flowers, but there are many varieties of different colors.

A. Johnsonii is one of the most common species; has red flowers broadly striped with white.

A. vittata has white flowers, with two red stripes on each segment. Of these there are many hybrids and varieties of rich coloring and extremely large flowers.

A. formosissima is a peculiar Mexican species, with deep, velvety, crimson flowers.

Vallota purpurea. Scarborough Lily, was formerly classed under the above genus. It is a handsome plant, with somewhat smaller rosy-red flowers. The plants should not be disturbed, as old-established plants flower best. Pot several bulbs together quite deeply in a large pot or pan, in rich soil, as for Amaryllis.

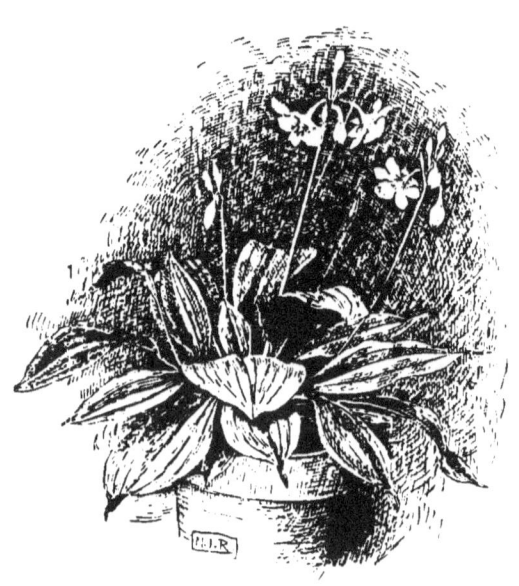

Amazon Lily. *Eucharis Amazonica.*

The Amazon lily, Eucharis Amazonica, is a tropical plant of great beauty, producing umbells of very large white flowers. It is easy of culture, but requires frequent washing and plenty of water during its season of growth. Bulbs should be planted deeply in rich, fibrous soil, and left undisturbed for years. Requires heat and moisture.

Crinum is a genus of very large bulbous plants, some of which are found wild in the South.

C. Amabile has leaves 3 to 4 feet in length, broad and soft. The flower scape rises above the arching leaves, with an umbell of numerous white fragrant flowers. Flowers in summer. Handsome on the veranda or in the hall.

C. capense and C. Americanum are two other desirable species. These should be grown in rich, fibrous soil in well-drained pots. They require plenty of water during the growing season and a partial rest in winter.

Hymenocallis. The Spider Lily, is a peculiar genus of desirable plants, with mostly white, sweet-scented flowers.

H. Andreana has a single large flower on a slender scape. Leaves long, strap-shaped.

H. rotata, a Florida plant with white flowers on a many-flowered scape. Flower-perianth with linear segments and large corona. A very interesting plant.

H. speciosa is a very handsome plant with pure white flowers. For culture see Crinum.

Imantophyllum miniatum is a striking plant of distichous habit, with long sword-shaped leaves, and umbells of about fifteen orange-red flowers borne on stout scapes. It is a plant with rootstock and fleshy roots, enjoys rich fibrous soil, with plenty of manure, and abundant water during the summer months. Large, well-established specimens are very ornamental for the hall or parlor. Enjoys partial shade.

I. cyrtanthiflorum is a species with smaller, not less elegant flowers.

Nerine. Guernsey Lily. A little genus of small, ornamental, bulbous plants with deciduous foliage. They require plenty of water during the growing season, after which they should be allowed to rest until the new growth begins to push. The soil should be rich and the pots well drained with crocks and broken pieces of charcoal.

N. sarniensis, with varieties of different colors from salmon to scarlet, and glowing crimson, is a very handsome autumn-flowering species.   These are somewhat similar to, but smaller than Amaryllis.

Zephyranthes rosea, when well grown, produces an abundance of handsome, erect, rosy-red flowers on single scapes.   The flowering time is spring.   Leaves linear, about 6 inches long. This is rather common in America.   It requires rich but a somewhat sandy soil and plenty of light and water while growing, and a partial rest afterward.

Scilla italica is a plant with a very large, greenish bulb, and long, arching leaves.   It is often seen in windows and is quite ornamental.   The flowers are insignificant.   It will grow well in ordinary soil with moderate watering.

Sanseviera. Bow-string Hemp. Plants with very stiff, narrow, erect, white-spotted foliage.   They are rather pretty foliage-plants and easily grown in rich soil.   They will do well in shade but require plenty of water and a warm position.

Yucca. Adam's needle, or Spanish Bayonette. Several plants of this genus are very useful for growing in vases, and a few are valuable pot-plants.

Y. aloefolia variegata has leaves striped with white, and is of a very regular habit.   The almost hardy, and hardy, forms are plentiful in parks and gardens, and although very beautiful when in flower, hardly suitable as window - plants in this country.   Y. recurva, with narrow, variegated leaves, is very handsome.

Yuccas should be grown in rich but gravelly soil, and can stand much rough treatment, plenty of sunshine and drought.

VII

ORCHIDS

THE strangest and most beautiful of all flowers are to be found in the Orchid family. Sometimes of immense size, they combine beauty of form with the most exquisite color, and are generally more or less fragrant. But they are not only remarkable on account of their outward form; the admirable construction of their organs of fertilization is wonderful without compare. The strange resemblance of many Orchid blossoms to birds, insects, and butterflies is also very remarkable. They depend on insects for their fertilization and reproduction, and the flowers produce plenty of honey in curiously constructed nectaries for the refreshment of their tiny visitors, which are of so great importance to them.

Orchids are mostly air-plants, living on trees in tropical and subtropical countries, and taking up their nutriment chiefly from the air by means of fleshy aërial roots. Fresh air is, therefore, a necessity to their growth. Many of these beautiful plants are extremely easy of culture, and several of the very best kinds will do well in a well-ventilated dwelling-house in sunny or half-shady positions. The stems and leaves are generally fleshy, of a grotesque and picturesque appearance. The genus Cypripedium, or Lady-slippers, has, however, very ornamental foliage springing directly from a crown of fleshy roots.

Most Orchids need a partial rest after the growing season. Their beautiful flowers appear, as a rule, during this period of rest.   When growth is finished, water should be given sparingly until the new growths appear.

The best material for growing Orchids is fibrous peat and fresh sphagnum moss, mixed in about equal proportions.   The pots, or pans, or baskets should be well drained by means of clean pieces of broken pots.   The fleshy roots will sometimes attach themselves to pots and baskets, and should, if possible, not be broken in re-potting.   Large pots should be avoided. During the period of growth copious watering is necessary, and in the case of Orchids grown in a dwelling-house, frequent washing of stems and leaves is very beneficial.

The varieties here recommended will do well in the ordi-

nary temperature of an apartment comfortable to live in, but they should not be grown in close, ill-ventilated, or excessively dry apartments.

Cattleya, a large and beautiful genus, stands foremost among the many types of popular Orchids. The flowers are very large with spreading petals, highly colored lip, and are sometimes produced in clusters of two or more. They last in perfection for a considerable time.

Cattleya Trianæ.

C. Trianæ is the most common species, varying in color from pure white to deep rosy-lilac, with a lip gorgeously blotched with orange and deep purple. It flowers during midwinter.

C. Mendelii produces large white flowers with purplish lip, somewhat later in the season.

C. Mossiæ flowers during the early summer months. The flowers are very large, varying in color from pale to deep rosy-lilac. The fringed lip is blotched with bright golden yellow.

C. Percivalliana blooms from late autumn to midwinter. The flowers are highly colored, the lip of a deep crimson-purple with orange veins.

Lælia is a genus nearly allied to Cattleya, but the flowers are considerably smaller in most species. L. Anceps is an autumn-flowering species producing loose spikes of rosy-purple flowers. It can be grown successfully on blocks of wood with a little moss and peat. L. Perrinii is a very fine species much resembling a Cattleya. It blooms during October and November. L. purpurata flowers in the spring, producing on stout erect peduncles several very large white flowers with crimson-purple lip.

Cœlogyne cristata is one of the finest winter-flowering orchids, with snowy-white flowers. The plant is very compact with narrow strap-shaped leaves, and when well grown will be almost covered with flowers at Christmas-time. It likes a cool, shady position and plenty of moisture, and should be grown in shallow pans.

Odontoglossums are very graceful plants from the Andes of South America, where they grow in high altitudes. The "Baby Orchid," O. grande, has large yellow flowers marked with brownish bars. Flowers in September and later. O. Rossi majus has white flowers with brown spots, appearing during the late winter months. These species should be grown in a cool and somewhat shady place, and must be given a thorough rest in winter.

Oncidium is a genus nearly allied to the last. The flowers are strange and beautiful, often produced in very large racemes.

The common Butterfly Orchid, Oncidium Papilio, is curious but not beautiful, and therefore not worth growing in a house. O. Forbesii is a beautiful plant with long arching racemes of copper-colored flowers edged with clear yellow. Blooms in the fall. O. varicosum and O. tigrinum have flowers borne on long arching peduncles; varicosum in ample branching racemes. The flowers are yellow, blotched and barred with chestnut-brown. The Oncidiums can be grown on blocks of wood or in baskets; they require good drainage if grown in pots, abundant water during growth, and moderate heat with a decided rest in winter.

Dendrobium nobile.

Dendrobium, a large East Indian genus, forms one of the most popular and useful families. The plants produce more or less long, terate or clavate stems, from the nodes of which the flowers are produced in clusters. They require plenty of heat and sun, a well-marked rest during winter, and plenty of water during the growing period. D. nobile is a very attractive and easily grown plant, with erect, fleshy stems of a finger's thickness, and a few lanceolate leaves at the apex. The flowers are produced in small clusters from ripe stems. The color is white-tinted lilac; lip crimson with deep maroon blotch in the throat. D. Wardianum has long arching stems and splendid white flowers; lip yellow in the centre with large,

deep crimson spots.   Flowers in profusion in early spring, and
is a very handsome plant.

Lycaste Skinnerii is one of the best Orchids for general use.
The long, broad, arching leaves are produced on ovate pseudo-
bulbs.   The flowers spring from the base of these and are produced singly on long peduncles.   They are large, of a more or
less deep purple color with darker lip ; sometimes white and

Lycaste Skinnerii.

then more valuable.   Grown in well-drained pots in a mixture of peat, small pieces of well - decayed cow manure, and
sphagnum moss.

Cypripedium.   The Lady's Slipper, is very easily grown.   It
has no pseudo-bulbs ; the leaves are more or less long, strap-
shaped or ensiform.   The foliage of some species is very handsome, of a silvery-gray color, blotched with deep green.   C.
insigne has long, green, strap-shaped leaves, and flowers of a

greenish-yellow, dotted and blotched with black. The upper sepal edged and striped with pure white. C. barbatum has handsome mottled leaves and large erect flowers. Upper sepal white with strong brown veins; lip blackish-purple; petals bordered with hairy glands. C. Lawrencianum is a very floriferous species of the same type as the above. Flowers of a brownish-green color with white dorsal sepal and black-purple veins.

C. Spicerianum is a still more beautiful species, yellowish-green with a broad white upper sepal with black veins.

Lady's Slipper.   *Cypripedium insigne.*

The Lady's Slippers can be grown on year after year without rest. They require a temperature of about 70 degrees, and plenty of moisture. Large specimen plants when in flower are very showy. With C. insigne flowering from December to March. C. barbatum from March to midsummer, and C. Spicerianum during the late autumn months, an almost continuous supply of flowers can be had from these species alone.

The above selection of Orchids have all been found to do well in dwelling-houses. They will perhaps, when better known, be more useful for this purpose than most other plants.

VIII

THE CALLA FAMILY

QUEER little Jack-in-the-Pulpit and his family form an interesting set of plants. They are chiefly re markable for their beautiful foliage, which is often richly and finely colored. There are some fine tropical climbers with fleshy stems and aërial roots, but most Aroids are low, herbaceous plants with succulent roots. The flowers are inconspicuous, disposed on a fleshy axis called a spathe, and protected by large colored bracts, which in the case of the com-mon Calla are white, and in the Fla-mingo plants deep scarlet. Some plants of this family, when flowering, emit a strong, disagreeable odor, and are therefore not desirable as house plants; others are of too delicate a nature, and require plenty of moisture.

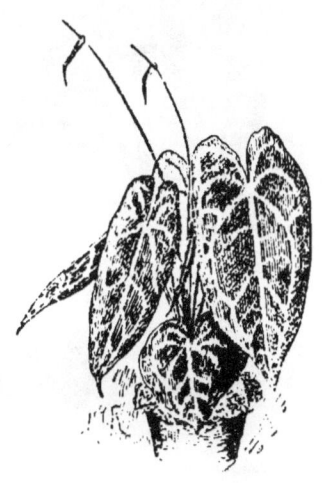

Anthurium crystallinum.

The Calla; Richardia œthio-pica, is one of the most useful plants for a house. It should be grown on steadily, summer and win-ter, but may be kept somewhat dry during the earlier winter months. Callas require rich soil and plenty of water during the summer. There are a couple of varieties considerably smaller than the common form. The

Yellow Calla is a fine plant with mottled leaves and pure yellow "flowers." There is another species with white flowers and white-spotted leaves. This latter can easily be grown from seeds, the others by means of offsets.

The Flamingo plant; Anthurium Scherzerianum, has "flowers" of a waxy texture and very bright scarlet color.

The leaves are leathery, ovate-lance-olate. The plant when in flower remains beautiful for a long period. Peaty, fibrous soil is most suitable for all Anthuriums.

Caladiums. Are very brightly colored foliage-plants. They lie dormant during winter, and should be left in the pots in a dry condition until starting. As soon as the young leaves begin to grow, the tubers should be potted in light sandy, humus-rich soil. Plenty of water should be given during the growing period. They last in beauty for a considerable time. When the color begins to fade, and the leaves lose their lustre, withdraw

Alocacia, macrohiza fol. var.

water gradually and keep the pots in a dry, cool place. C. arzyritis is a dwarf form with white-veined foliage.

The Alocacias can be treated in a similar way, but may also be kept growing all the year round. The leaves are of great variety, some of an almost metallic appearance, others bright green or variegated with white. They are mostly broadly hastate or shield-like in outline. A. metallica, macrohiza variegata, and Sanderiana, are fine, desirable forms.

Anthurium crystallinum is a plant of similar appearance. It has large, cordate leaves about a foot and a half long, with a glistening surface and white ribs.

Curmeria Wallisii. This is a very compact and beautiful plant, with ovate leathery leaves, finely spotted green and yellow. Requires heat and moisture for its development, hence it is best for a terrarium when grown as a house plant. Propagated by division, and grown in rich, fibrous soil.

Dieffenbachia.

Diffenbachia is the name of a number of plants with yellow-spotted leaves. They form a slender stem, and are graceful and ornamental. They are best suitable for the South, but can also be grown in the North in double windows or in large glass cases.

Philodendrum verucosum. This is a curious little climbing plant, with fleshy stems and numerous air-roots. The leaves are cordate in outline, of a velvety lustre, deep olive-green. A neat little subject for a terrarium. Will grow in peat and moss, and requires constant heat and moisture.

Phyllotœnium Lindenii is the best foliage-plant of this class forming masses of fine variegated leaves. The leaf is hastate in outline, quite large, white in the middle and along the principal veins.

All Aroids like rich vegetable soil and a partially shaded position. They are easily grown plants, propagated by means of seeds or division of the rootstock, or by cuttings.

Phyllotænium Lindenii

The species here described love heat and moisture. The warmest place in the house should be reserved for them. A suitable bay-window or a terrarium is best for nearly all plants of this family.

The Phyllotænium and the common Calla may be grown almost anywhere, and will do well in ordinary rich, fibrous soil.

IX

THE PINE-APPLE FAMILY

ALL plants of this family are of a peculiar stiff and rigid appearance. The majority are air-plants, living as Epiphytes in dense tropical woods, where the exquisite beauty of their flowers is seldom seen by human eyes. Some have no roots, but exist through nutriment taken up directly from the air. In flowering the main plant generally dies, leaving several young ones around its base to continue the struggle for existence. The flowers appear in terminal spikes, and are protected by bracts, which are sometimes highly colored. Most of these plants are grown exclusively for the beauty of their foliage, which is often curiously spotted, mottled, or veined. No plants can be more indifferent to outward conditions; moisture or drought, sunshine or shadow, seem to be equally acceptable. In cultivation they require only little soil, composed of peat, moss, and charcoal, but plenty of water is beneficial. All can be propagated by means of seeds or offsets. Seeds should be sown in shallow pans in peaty soil, covered by glass, and kept moist and somewhat shady in a temperature of about seventy degrees. The best kinds for general use are:

Achmea fulgens. Leaves broadly strap-shaped, curving, parallel-veined. Flowers on erect scapes from the centre of the plant in a close terminal panicle. Flowers scarlet, with bluish segments.

Billbergia nutans is a handsome winter-flowering plant. Leaves long, strap-shaped, spiny, spreading. Flowers red and yellow, in long loose spikes, on slender nodding peduncles, bracts red. Grow in light, rich soil in pots.

Bromelia Ananas variegata. Pine-apple with variegated leaves is a very handsome foliage-plant. The leaves are green, with broad bands of white, suffused with crimson. Very valuable for vases and as a common window plant. Fine for table decoration. Soil as for Billbergia.

Massangea hieroglyphica is like an Achmea in appearance, with finely tessallated leaves, green with almost black, irregular bars. This is a very neat and attractive plant.

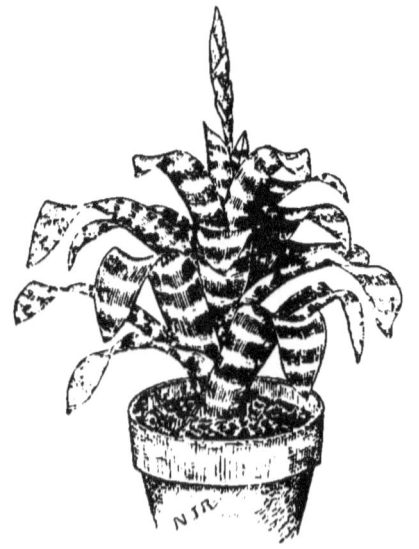

Tillandsia splendens.

Tillandsia, to which genus the Florida air-plant and the Spanish moss belong, consists mainly of Epiphytes very dissimilar in appearance. T. psittacina has short, strap-shaped, slightly curving foliage. Flowers in a short spike with scarlet

bracts.   T. pulchra is another kind with pretty flowers.
T. splendens, has the foliage barred with almost black, regular
spots.

Most of the foregoing species can be grown on blocks of
wood, or in baskets in peat and moss as recommended for Orchids.   They should be kept moist during summer, and have
a thorough rest in winter.   When well grown and kept clean and
free from dust, they are highly ornamental, and useful for table
decoration.

A terrarium or double window will suit all, but even in the
most arid atmosphere and under the most adverse conditions
they generally do well, provided watering is not overdone.

X

PALMS

PALMS are tropical plants of great beauty. Their large leaves are borne on slender, simple stems, which often rise to a considerable height, a picture of lightness and elegance. The stems sometimes divide at the base and form bushy specimens, as is always the case with the very common and very beautiful *Areca lutescens* and a few of our own dwarf palms. The leaves are often of a gigantic size, reaching a length of thirty or forty feet, and a width of five. The smaller forms are most desirable for house culture, as they remain at a convenient size for years. Even in a small state, when clean and healthy, palms are very ornamental. Some have feather-veined leaves, long, graceful, arching; in others, as in the common Fan palm, the leaves are palmately veined.

Nearly all palms can be grown successfully in this country, but they require a warm temperature for quick development. In a dwelling-house they make but little growth during the winter months, and the plants should then be kept considerably dryer than during the extreme heat of summer, when liberal waterings are needed.

This class of plants cannot be propagated in an apartment with any degree of success. Healthy specimens should be bought when desired, and if properly cared for will form permanent additions to a collection of plants. The leaves should be kept clean by means of sponging and washing.

Palms require rich, fibrous soil, and plenty of water; they can, however, remain in comparatively small pots for years,

Areca lutescens.

and will, under certain conditions, grow and flourish with apparently no sustenance except water. In re-potting palms the roots should not be disturbed or torn, or buried in too great a mass of soil. The drainage must be good, and for small and tender species pieces of broken charcoal mixed with the soil is beneficial. Large palms may be left undisturbed for years, provided the top soil is occasionally replaced by new and very rich top-dressing. Artificial manures containing plenty of nitrogenous matter, sheep manure, bone and blood, or fish-guano are very good for this purpose. All palms, large and small, are equally benefited by liberal doses of liquid manure. Most of the species commonly grown do best in warm, half-shady positions, for although the sun is very beneficial to them, it is very liable to burn and disfigure the leaves.

Some palms lift themselves above the soil on strong, woody roots. This is a natural tendency which should be taken notice of when potting. No species should be planted very deep in the soil.

A few of the best kinds for general use are, among pinnately veined palms :

Areca lutescens, a very attractive bushy palm, with long and graceful leaves on slender stems. The petioles of the leaves are of a bright orange-yellow spotted brown. The leaves are erect, slightly curving. Large, bushy specimens are very ornamental. There are several other Arecas, all distinguished by means of the color of the leaves. as the red Areca, the white Areca, and others. They are all valuable plants.

Cocos Weddeliana is a very small palm, with finely pinnated leaves. It is a good subject for a terrarium, and one of the best palms for table decoration. It requires plenty of heat and moisture, and the foliage is benefited by frequent spray-ings. A mixture of fibrous peat and loam, with some addition of well-rotted cow manure and sand, makes a very suitable soil. This palm should be grown in comparatively small, well-drained pots.

Chamadoreas are small, elegant palms, with slender stems and large crowns of long pinnate leaves. They never grow too large for a room, are ornamental, and easily grown in rich, fibrous soil. A partial shade and liberal watering is needed in summer.

Kentia is a genus of palms almost similar to the Arecas in habit when small. They are robust-growing plants, with long, arching leaves, and among the best of all pinnately leaved palms. They require rich soil and liberal watering.

Fan Palm. *Livistona sinensis.*

Phœnix is the botanical name of the large Date-palm family. These, when small, are very useful and will stand lots of rough treatment. They have a very bushy, feathery appearance on account of their long, spreading leaves, which are somewhat stiff and spiny at the base. Plenty of light and air is beneficial to all; liberal watering and full exposure to the sun is best for the stronger kinds, and they are peculiarly well adapted for lawn decoration in summer.

The species most suitable for a house is Ph. rupicola; it has long and finely pinnate leaves, and is the most graceful one of the genus. Ph. tennis and Ph. canariensis are common and ornamental kinds.

Ptychosperma resemble Kentias and Arecas in many respects. The two species commonly grown, Pt. Cunninghamii and Pt. Alexandræ, are of about equal value.

Verschaffeltia splendida is a palm of a very striking appearance. The leaves are broad, scarcely pinnate in young specimens, and of a fine reddish color. The stem is slender and very spiny, and is supported on strong woody roots. This species requires a fibrous and somewhat peaty soil, and plenty of heat and atmospheric moisture. It is best suited to the South.

The Royal Palm (Oreodoxa regia) and the Wax-palm (Ceroxylon), as also the Fish-tail palm (Caryota), are other beautiful pinnately leaved species.

Fan-palms are so named because their foliage resembles a fan in outline. The best are:

The European Fan-palm, Chamærops humilis, a fine species, with silvery-gray leaves. It forms elegant spreading specimens. The tall-growing form, Ch. exelsa, is also very ornamental. They enjoy rich, well-drained soil and plenty of moisture during the hot season.

The Chinese Fan-palm, Livistona Chinensis, is the most popular palm grown. It is of a compact and robust habit, and a rapid grower. There are several other species of this genus, very beautiful, but as yet little known.

Licuala grandis is a newly introduced, very ornamental palm, with almost orbicular leaves of deep-green color. It is smaller and more compact than the Livistona, and quite different in appearance, but very beautiful.

Rhapis flabelliformis has small palmate leaves on numerous slender stems. It forms erect, bushy specimens, and will do well in a shady position. Among other Fan-palms are *Thrinax* and *Washingtonia*—the first a very elegant palm, the last

Rhapis flabelliformis.

rather coarse and not satisfactory for house culture in this country.

The general cultural notes given above apply to all species here described.

XI

DRACÆNAS, SCREW-PINES, AND SAGO-PALMS

 ESIDES Palms there are numbers of plants having a palm-like appearance, and serving much the same purpose when cultivated. Among these are the *Carludovicas*, plants with fan-shaped leaves on long, slender stalks. They should be grown in rich, fibrous soil, and require more water than most palms.

Curculigo, a small but handsome plant, has broad, lanceolate, plicate leaves, growing from a thick creeping stem. There is a fine variety with white-variegated leaves. This also requires good rich soil and plenty of water.

Of the *Banana family* several kinds are of neat habit and quite ornamental. They are very rapid growers, but are seldom grown except in conservatories.

Heliconia aureo-striata is a beautiful and useful plant of this class. It is a plant of a dwarf and compact habit, and has fine green leaves, obliquely striped with golden yellow. This plant will do well in a half-shady and warm position. Like all plants of its class, it requires the richest of soils and abundant watering during summer. During winter it should be kept rather dry.

The Screw-pines, Pandanus, when young are very handsome plants, especially the beautifully variegated form known as Pandanus Veitchii. Small specimens of this are very useful for table decoration. When grown in a house, a bay-window is the best place, but it will also do well in any warm, light, and airy room. The Screw-pines do well in a mixture of equal

Dracena terminalis variety.

parts of fibrous loam and peat, with a slight addition of sharp sand and some decayed manure. The pots must be well drained, and broken charcoal mixed in the soil is to be recommended.   Careful watering, rather liberal in the summer-time and restricted during winter, is essential.

Dracæna is a large genus of very ornamental plants, with long, arching, strap-shaped or lanceolate leaves on slender stems.   Some kinds are very highly colored, having dark bronzy leaves striped with various shades of white and red and yellow, spotted, mottled, or variegated.   Numerous hybrids have been raised in European gardens, which, when well grown, are extremely fine.   Dracænas are generally of a neat, compact habit, useful for table and other decorations. They are increased by means of cuttings taken from old stems laid down in sand, but they cannot be easily propagated in a dwelling-house.   The soil should be composed of equal parts of fibrous loam, leaf mould, and well-decayed manure, with a liberal addition of sharp sand.   Plenty of water and frequent spraying, or washing, of the foliage is beneficial.   In a house where spraying is impracticable washing is the best, and a good sponging of the leaves at regular intervals will be necessary to prevent insects and diseases.   The position should be a half-shady one in a double window or a warm room.

Some of the best varieties are :   D. indivisa, with long, arching, strap-shaped leaves.   This is a useful plant for vases and window-boxes ; it is hardier than the rest and will do well in a cool place.

D. imperialis has broad, slightly recurved leaves, which are striped with crimson, white, and pink.   D. Baptistii is a brightly colored variety, with the leaves striped yellow and dull red.   D. magnifica has very broad leaves of a bronzy-green color, slightly striped with white and pale green.   D. Regina is one of the finest and best, with broad, deep-green leaves bordered with pure white.   D. terminalis is a species with numerous varieties and hybrids, all highly colored. Fine hybrid forms are : D. Amabilis, leaves striped green and yellow. D. Hendersonii, leaves curiously mottled and striped with white and lilac.

D. fragrans belongs to a different type of plants, with rather broad and very long, recurved, and spreading leaves. Of this there are two or three varieties with the leaves striped yellow. The best and hardiest of these is D. Massangeana. The finest is D. Lindenii.

These plants are as yet little known in America, but they do well in a

Dracena Regina.

house when properly treated, and no plants can be better suitable for the decoration of a house.

Sago-Palms are of many different kinds. All have very ornamental leaves spreading from the crown of thick scaly stems. There is no class of plants better suited to house culture, as the hard texture of the leaves renders them proof against injuries of any kind. They will do well in almost any position, but prefer a warm place and plenty of water in summer. The young leaves are at first tender, but become firm in a very short time. Among these :

Cycas revoluta is the kind most commonly grown, and the best in every way. The leaves are from 2 to 4 feet long, and about 6 or 8 inches wide, very closely pinnate and deep, glossy green.   C. circinalis is a variety considerably larger, but just as beautiful.   Of smaller kinds the small Florida Sago-palm, **Zamia integrifolia,** is quite common in cultivation.   The leaflets of this species are broad and somewhat hairy.

The soil should be the same as that recommended for Palms, and the treatment after establishment is practically the same. Sago-palms will do well in comparatively small pots.   For lawn decoration in summer, or for large halls or parlors, they are invaluable.

XII

FERNS AND MOSSES

ERNS are universally known and admired for the beauty of their foliage. The family consists of a great number of species, mostly herbaceous, but sometimes of gigantic size, with palm-like stems and ample crowns of graceful foliage ; others tiny, delicate things, with fronds of a transparent, film-like texture.

Most ferns will grow in shade. They are generally moisture-loving plants, growing in the depths of woods and forests among leaves and decaying vegetable matter. Some few species grow in the crevices of rocks in sunny and exposed positions, and should be treated accordingly when grown. The marvellous golden and silvery leaved ferns are of this nature. To grow ferns successfully a liberal drainage should be provided for ; a rich vegetable soil, consisting of equal parts of fibrous loam, leaf mould, and sand, will suit most species. For golden and silvery leaved ferns one-fourth part of old mortar is beneficial. The watering must be liberal in the growing season, but the foliage should, as a rule, be kept absolutely dry ; but if dirty the leaves may be cleaned in the ordinary way—by washing. An even and moderate temperature is best suitable to all species commonly grown. The shadier positions in the house are best ; no fern should be exposed to the full rays of the sun.

Many ferns can be successfully grown in Wardian cases or terrariums in any ordinary house. Among species best suited for this purpose many of the finer Maiden-hair ferns take the first place. The filmy ferns, also, such as the Trichomanes and Hymenophyllum, are, because of their delicate beauty, very suitable. They should be planted among moss and peat on old pieces of wood, and kept moist and shady.

The Maiden-hair ferns, or Adiantums, have usually very

Maiden-hair Fern. *Adiantum Farleyense.*

finely divided leaves, the common one growing in rocky woods is a typical species. The A. Farleyense is considered the most beautiful of the whole family. It has broad doubly pinnate hanging fronds which are very finely fringed. It cannot stand the dry atmosphere of a room for any length of time, but can be grown successfully in a glass case. A. cuneatum and the large-growing A. formosum are more hardy.

The Shield ferns; Aspidium Lastrea. So named from the

appearance of the shield-like fruit-spots on the back of the leaves, are firmer in texture and will do well with little care. The best are : A. falcatum, with long pinnate fronds of a glossy deep-green appearance. A. amabile, with broader, twice pinnate leaves almost triangular in outlines. Lastrea aristata variegata has finely variegated foliage, and is one of the best ferns for a dwelling-room.

Spleen-wort ; Asplenium. This is the name of a large family of ferns. A. bulbiferum, as also A. flaccidum, has large finely

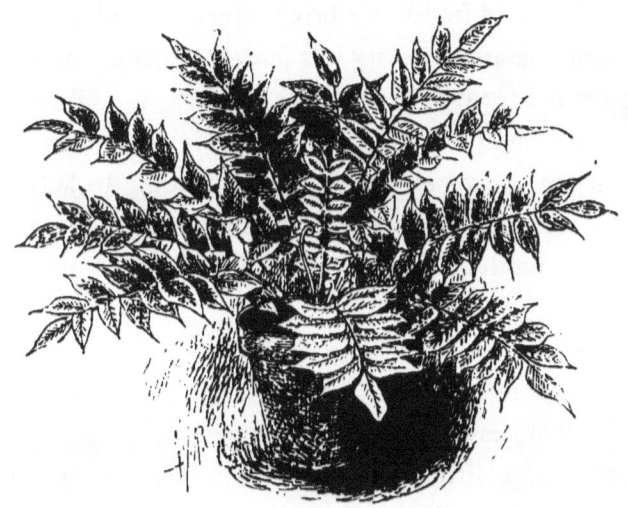

Aspidium (Cyrtomium) falcatum.

divided leaves. Small plants are produced in abundance on the fronds, giving the plant a peculiar appearance. These are very beautiful and well adapted for room culture. So is also the more hardy A. lucidum, with pinnate shining leaves.

Davallias, or Hare's-foot ferns, have creeping stems clothed with gray hair-like scales. Ample, mostly triangular fronds spring at irregular intervals from these. They are of a firm texture and will therefore stand a dry atmosphere. Some of the smaller kinds can be grown in baskets and are very pretty. The best are: D. canariensis and D. stricta. For these plenty of peat should be used with the soil.

The Gold- and Silver-ferns; Gymnogramme. These are remarkable on account of their foliage being powdered with white or yellow dust on the lower side. They are strikingly beautiful when well grown. During their period of rest in winter, water must be given very sparingly.

Lomaria gibba is a fern commonly seen in green-houses; it has long pinnatifid fronds of a bright green. Good, rich soil, and liberal watering are necessary to a fine development of this plant.

The Sword-ferns; Nephrolepis. These do well in a house, and are the most common ferns in American green-houses. They can be grown either in pots or hanging baskets. Long cord-like runners or *stolons* are produced from the base of the stem; these produce plantlets by which all sword-ferns may be increased.

Nephrodium is a very large genus, of which N. molle is the most common representant. There is a fine-fringed variety of this. Both are easily increased by means of spores.

Onychium, a little Japanese fern, is very hardy, and feels quite at home in a shady corner in a room. The foliage is finely divided, dark green, and firm in texture.

The Eagle-ferns; Pteris, are quite numerous, some have large, rich foliage, others have pinnate leaves with strap-shaped segments. Pt. argyrea and Pt. tremula are both very ornamental. The first has foliage variegated with silvery gray, the tremula has deep green, triangular leaves. Pt. serrulata cristata, Pt. cretica, and albo-lineata are all neat, and of firm texture and graceful habit. These are well adapted for planting in vases, baskets, or inside window-boxes.

The Filmy Ferns above mentioned are very numerous. They are sometimes very minute, of a moss-like appearance, and are, when cultivated in a moist atmosphere, always covered with dew. They are among the most remarkable plants known, exceedingly beautiful, with fronds of almost hair-like appearance. They must be grown in a glass-case or terrarium.

Pteris argyrea.

Club mosses are suitable for the same purpose as filmy ferns. Some are tender and creeping and form dense masses on the ground; others are erect and of a robust habit. None are common in cultivation, but they deserve mention in connection with the terrarium. All require a moist atmosphere and should be grown in rich vegetable, somewhat sandy soil.

XIII

MISCELLANEOUS FLOWERING PLANTS

**butilon.** Flowering maple. This is a genus of fine green-house shrubs with pendant, bell-shaped flowers of various colors. Propagated by means of cuttings of growing wood inserted in sand. The soil should be rich and fibrous, composed of equal parts loam, leaf-mould, and well-decayed manure with some addition of sharp sand. Abutilons grow rapidly and will bloom when quite small. There are varieties with crimson, yellow, rose-colored, and white flowers. To form bushy plants the young shoots should be nipped occasionally.

Acacia. Acacias when in flower are exceedingly beautiful plants, and many besides have fine foliage. Propagate by means of half-ripe cuttings taken with a slant and inserted in sand, in a pot which should be covered with a pane of glass and kept in a warm, shady place. Soil for Acacias should consist of equal parts fibrous loam and leaf-mould, or peat with plenty of sand. They must be potted firmly.

There are some kinds with numerous globular heads of flowers, others have the flowers disposed in long spikes from the axils of the leaves or phyllodea. The Silver Wattle of Australia, Acacia dealbata, is an extremely fine tree with handsome leaves and an abundance of pale yellow blossoms. Drummond's Acacia, the armed Acacia, the linear-leaved Acacia, all are very desirable kinds. A. Lophanta has very large doubly pinnate leaves, and is quite ornamental as a small plant.

Achimenes are small plants of the Gloxinia family, with tender trailing stems and very pretty flowers of all colors. They are very floriferous, of a herbaceous habit and tuberous-rooted. The tubers should be planted in March or April in light sandy soil. After planting and thorough watering the plants should be brought into a pretty warm room and kept in a shady position until started. In two months the plants will bloom freely. When stems and flowers decay store the pots in a cool, dry place till the following spring.

Agathea. This is a shrubby plant with blue aster-like flowers. Propagate by cuttings under glass, if handy. To form bushy specimens pinch often. Grows quickly and will do well in ordinary soil and in a cool place.

Ageratum. An almost hardy plant of a neat compact habit, producing numerous blue flowers. Useful for baskets and window-boxes. Cuttings root freely.

Alyssum maritimum. This is a plant commonly known by the simple name of Sweet Alyssum. It is a low, compact plant, producing dense racemes of small, white, sweet-scented flowers. Propagated by brittle cuttings in sand in a warm, shady place; it will grow well in any ordinary soil. Useful for planting in baskets and window-boxes.

Azaleas are beautiful evergreen shrubs of a bushy habit. There are double and single varieties, crimson, salmon-colored, white, one-colored or striped. Azaleas are very floriferous and, when brought into flower early in spring, very useful and beautiful plants. They should be kept in a cool and somewhat shady position in summer, and must never be allowed to get dry. Soil composed of fibrous peat and sand suits them best. Potting should be done very firmly, especially in the case of young plants. Azaleas do best in cool and airy apartments. If they are intended for forcing, they should be brought into a warmer place and sprayed frequently until the flowers expand.

Boronia megastigma. A beautiful slender plant, with axillary purple flowers in great profusion in early spring. Very sweet scented. Leaves small, pinnate, or tri-foliate. Boronias should be grown in a soil composed of equal parts of fibrous loam, peat, leaf mould, and sand, and need firm potting, plenty of water at the root during summer, and a light, airy position in a cool place.

Bouvardias. Well-known plants, producing clusters of brilliant flowers. Propagate by means of half-ripe cuttings, and pot in light fibrous soil. Water freely in summer and keep in a light, cool place. Repot frequently, and stop the young growths as often as necessary to form bushy plants. Occasional sprayings are beneficial. Bouvardias flower for a long period in winter, spring, and early summer. There are single and double flowers, white, flesh-colored, or scarlet.

Browallias are annual plants with showy blue and white flowers, and very pretty when in bloom. Sow seeds in summer, in light sandy soil. Cover the seed-pot with a pane of glass; keep moist and shady, thin the seedlings and pot later singly in small pots. Grow the plants on in rich fibrous soil, and pinch frequently to form bushy specimens for winter-blooming.

Camellia. This old favorite, although hardy in the South, deserves to be grown in a small state as a window-plant in the North. Procure small bushy plants of a flowering size. Repot about once in two years, in a mixture of equal parts of fibrous loam, leaf-mould peat and sand. Water liberally in summer and keep the plants in a cool place. Prune long shoots when necessary to keep the plants bushy. Small pots are best; firm potting is essential. The flowers expand in winter and keep beautiful a long time. To avoid the falling of buds water carefully and never allow the roots to dry. Spray occasionally.

Canna. The new French Cannas are exceedingly fine, and may be had in bloom in a sunny apartment for a long period of the winter. They require large pots and very rich soil, with a liberal supply of water. The colors of many of the Crozy varieties are exceedingly showy.

Streptosolon jamesonii.

Choysya is the name of a neat, shrubby plant with trifoliate leaves and terminal racemes of white fragrant flowers. Propagate by half-ripe cuttings in spring. Grow in ordinary soil in a light and cool position.

Chorizema. Plants of the pea-family, with numerous red and yellow flowers. They will thrive in equal parts of loam and peat with the usual admixture of sand. Propagate by seeds or cuttings. Train carefully to make bushy plants. When well grown, and in full bloom in early spring, nothing can be more beautiful.

Citrus. Orange. These can be grown in pots, and will flower and fruit tolerably well, but soon grow too large for a house. The Otaheite-Orange is a variety of neat and compact habit, flowers freely as a small plant, and with good training forms a nice specimen. Propagate by seeds in sandy soil. repot several times the first year.   Rich fibrous soil should be used after a while, and top-dressings of artificial manures are very beneficial for flowering plants.   Requires liberal watering and occasional sprayings.

Cigar-plant.   Cuphea.   This is a well-known dwarf flowering plant, producing numerous cylindrical flowers all the year round.   It is excellent for vases and window-boxes, and especially useful in the summer-time for outdoor display.   Propagate by cuttings, which root easily.

Cytisus is a handsome, bushy, floriferous plant of the pea-family.   It is capable of being trained into very compact specimens.   Flowers yellow in long racemes.   There are several varieties, all valuable.   The propagation is difficult and slow in a house, but plants are cheap.   Rich fibrous loam with one-third leaf-mould and sand makes a suitable soil.   Young plants should be trimmed two or three times a year to form bushy specimens ; they flower late in spring.

Datura Arborea.   Trumpet-flower.   This is a straggling, soft-wooded shrub, with large oblong leaves and enormous hanging, trumpet-like flowers, white, slightly tinged with violet, single or double.   It is curious and picturesque, and forms a nice plant for the lawn.   It can be kept in a cool cellar during the winter.   Propagate by soft-wooded cuttings.

Epacris is a genus of Heath-like plants producing terminal spikes of brightly colored flowers.   They are better adapted for American culture than the Cape Heaths, being able to stand more heat and moisture.   Propagation easy, but slow, by means of cuttings.   Young plants should be procured for home-growing.   Good, fibrous, peaty soil is most suitable.   Potting and watering must be done with care. and good drainage is of great importance.   The long, erect shoots on strong plants should not be stopped, as these when ripe produce the flowers of the season. A half-shady position is best. The following garden varieties are recommended : hyacinthiflora alba, white; fulgens, scarlet ; carminata, carmine ; ignea, fiery red.

Erica. Cape Heaths. These are not often seen in American gardens ; in Europe they are very important decorative plants for house and home. There is a great number of species, producing more or less showy, often fragrant, flowers. The propagation in a house is slow, and it is therefore best to procure small flowering plants from a florist. They require the same soil and treatment as Epacris, but all long shoots should be nipped in order to make the plants bushy. Firm potting, careful watering, and good drainage are essential. For watering Cape Heaths and Epacris soft water is preferable. The following are a few of the best : E. Cavendishii, yellow ; E. caffra, small white flowers, very numerous, fragrant ; E. hyemalis, pink and white flowers ; E. persoluta and P. alba, with small red or white flowers ; E. ventricosa, long, tubular flowers in umbels, purple ; E. vestita and its numerous varieties. These are only a few of the more important forms. All Ericas and Epacri ought to prove hardy in the Southern States.

Erythrinas, or Coral-trees, are extremely showy plants of the pea-family, hardy in the South. They have trifoliate, sometimes variegated leaves, and some species make fine foliage plants. The flowers, produced in long terminal racemes, are coral-red or scarlet. The plants may be wintered in a dry state in a cellar, and should be repotted early in the season. Water should at first be given moderately, but very liberally later in the spring as the plants develop. After flowering, prune back to within a few inches of the stem. The object is to produce strong, ripe shoots for flowering the following season.

The *Cherokee beans*, E. crista-galli and E. herbacea, produce flowers on herbaceous shoots the first season and flower early in the fall.

E. indica Parcellii is a fine tree with beautiful white-variegated foliage. This one is ornamental all the year round, and should not be allowed to dry. All Erythrinas can be propagated by means of seeds and cuttings. Rich, fibrous soil, and plenty of water.

Euphorbia. Milkwort. Spurge. These are curious sometimes cactus-like plants, almost leafless, with globular and fleshy stems. The only species deserving wider culture is the common Poinsettia : E. pulcherima, and E. splendens, both of which are hardy in the South. The Poinsettia is grown for the sake of the splendid scarlet bracts produced beneath the flowers. These measure often a foot in length and are very showy. Poinsettias for winter-flowering should be grown in small pots and kept dwarf by means of moderate watering and plenty of air. The propagation takes place in summer by means of cuttings of young shoots. They root easily enough under glass in sharp sand with moderate watering. Equal parts of fibrous loam, leaf mould, decayed manure, and sand make a good soil.

After rooting, the plants should be potted and grown as rapidly as possible to produce a crown of large colored bracts in mid-winter. These remain beautiful a long time. After flowering, a few months of rest is generally given. The culture of E. splendens and E. fulgens is too difficult to be here recommended.

Gardenias, or Cape Jessamines, are well-known plants whose exquisite beauty is fully seen in some of the Southern States, where the plant is hardy. Gardenias grow easily from half-ripe cuttings, and require liberal watering and rich fibrous soil. As pot-plants they must be sprayed or washed often. A slight rest in the fall to ripen the young growth is beneficial. The plants, if well ripened, produce quantities of large, double, fragrant flowers of a milky white color.

The Gesnera- or **Gloxinia-family** is a very beautiful one. Numerous species with brilliant flowers and fine foliage are common in cultivation. A number of these plants grow from fleshy tubers or stolons, and need absolute rest for a certain period of the year. Others grow and remain ornamental all the year round. All can be propagated by means of seeds and cuttings, or by the division of tubers. They should be grown in well-drained pots in equal parts of loam, leaf-mould, and a mixture of peat and sand. They require liberal watering and a shady position during the growing season. Those needing rest should be stored away in a dry, cool place, after flowering, and the tubers must be cleaned and repotted in spring as early as growth commences. After potting and watering old tubers, keep in a warm and shady position ; remove gradually to a cooler and lighter place. *Tydea, Naegelia, Isoloma,* and *Gesnera* are typical mostly tuberous-rooted plants of this family. These and other Gesneraceæ may be started at different times of the year to produce a succession of flowers. The Gesnera family is almost unsurpassed in richly colored flowers, neat habit, and easy culture.

Hibiscus, or **Chinese rose,** is one of the most gorgeous green-house plants, and when small and bushy is one of the best for house-culture. Propagated by cuttings of young wood and grown rapidly in rich fibrous soil, it soon reaches a flowering size. It requires large pots and plenty of moisture during the growing season. There are varieties of many colors, single or double.   The variety Cooperii is a fine foliage plant with richly colored leaves.

Hydrangea (H. hortensis) is a pretty well known plant, less successfully grown in America than it deserves to be.   In this country it requires a half-shady position.   Propagated by cuttings of young shoots, any time of the year, but preferably in spring.   Young plants should be pushed on rapidly in rich soil, and must be gradually brought to rest in the fall, after which less water should be given.   The plants should not lose their leaves, but may be kept in a cool, light cellar until after Christmas, when repotting can be done if necessary.   The plants must then be cleaned and brought into a slightly warmer place. Liberal watering and spraying will soon develop the dormant buds.   The plants may also be kept in a cool, shady window all the year round, but will then flower later. The presence of alum or iron in the soil will change the originally red flowers into a beautiful blue.

Jacobinia Ghiesbreghtiana.

The Acanthus Family contains a number of handsome flowering, suffruticose plants : *Jacobinia Ghiesbreghtiana*, producing fine scarlet flowers in axillar racemes, is one of the finest. *Peristrophe speciosa*, with long ringent flowers of a pale rosy-pink produced in great number. *Libonia floribunda*, a neat, bushy plant, with ovate leaves and numerous tubular, scarlet flowers. *Streptosolon Jamesonii*, with the habit of a Libonia, producing umbels of rather large yellow and red flowers. *Justitia carnea*, a rather coarse, upright-growing plant, with heads of long, ringent flowers. *The genus Eranthemum* is rich both in handsome foliage and flowering plants.

All the above are well suited to window-culture. They are easily propagated by means of cuttings inserted in light soil, singly in small pots, and kept in a glass case until rooted. Rich, but fibrous and sandy, soil is good for all, and a half-shady position is best during the summer months. The young plants should be pinched sufficient to form bushy specimens, which will flower during the winter.

Lantanas are pretty plants of the Verbena family. They produce umbels of showy flowers and are popular for bedding and for window-boxes. Propagated any time of the year when there is suitable young wood for cuttings. Lantanas require rich, fibrous soil.

Linum trigynum.

Linum trigynum. Yellow flax. A handsome and floriferous plant for winter flowering. For culture, see Jacobinia (Acanthus family).

Mahernia, a small, floriferous plant, with slender branches and sweet-scented Oxalis-like flowers. It grows best in light, fibrous soil, and should be propagated by means of young herbaceous cuttings. The plants must be carefully trimmed and tied to form fine specimens. The yellow blossoms expand shortly after midwinter. The plants should have a gentle rest after flowering, after which they may be pruned back, repotted, and started afresh.

Mignonette can easily be raised in pots for winter use. Sow a few seeds of some good variety in small pots, thin the seedlings, and leave the strongest only. Repot in rich soil once or twice. Keep the plants growing in a cool, airy room, and pinch the shoots to form bushy plants. Water freely and spray or dip the top occasionally in water. The plants need staking.

Musk-plant. Mimulus moschatus. Can be grown from seed in the spring for baskets and window-boxes. It is a pretty dwarf plant, with numerous yellow flowers of a musky odor.

Myrtles can be grown with the greatest of ease in almost any house. They are propagated by means of cuttings taken with a heal, any time of the year, and grow well in a soil composed of equal parts fibrous loam, leaf-mould, decayed manure, and sand. Trim the young plants as they grow with a pair of scissors to form bushy specimens. Large plants will flower freely.

Nerium Oleander. To grow the Oleander successfully, propagate by means of ripe cuttings inserted in water through the cork of a bottle. The soil recommended for myrtles will suit oleanders just as well. Water freely during the growing period. If placed in the open air in summer the branches will ripen well and produce flowers freely during fall and winter. If the roots are allowed to dry suddenly the young buds are apt to drop off. Injury to the roots through bad drainage will produce the same effect. The leaves and flowers of the Oleander are very poisonous.

Olea fragrans. American Olive. This is an evergreen plant of a fine bushy habit and holly-like leaves. It produces a quantity of small, white, fragrant flowers. Propagation rather slow, by means of cuttings. Hardy in the South.

Oxalis. These are tuberous-rooted plants with trifoliate leaves and very pretty flowers of different colors. Bulbs should be procured early in spring, planted in light sandy soil, and kept moist and shady until starting. Some kinds will rest after flowering, others continue to grow and blossom almost throughout the year.

Pansies, for winter use, can easily be grown in pots or shallow boxes in any room not too cool. Seed should be sown in September.

Pleroma macrantha is an exceedingly beautiful shrub of the Melastoma family. It has oblong, hairy leaves, slender stems, and very large and beautiful flowers of a purplish-blue color. It will grow well in a soil composed of equal parts fibrous loam, peat, well-decayed manure, and sand. A fine plant for the South. When grown as a house-plant in the North a sunny position is necessary.

Polygala speciosa and other kinds are very handsome winter-flowering plants, producing long racemes of white or purple flowers. Leaves small, linear. To be grown in a mixture of equal parts leaf-mould, peat, and sand. Propagation easy by means of half-ripe cuttings. These plants must be potted very firmly.

Primula obconica is a handsome winter-blooming Primrose, producing umbels of large lilac flowers on tall peduncles, and

fine cordate leaves.   Seeds should be sown early in spring.
Seedlings repricked in a soil composed of equal parts of loam,
leaf-mould, decayed manure, and sand will grow rapidly.
They should be grown in a cool, airy place, and must be repotted frequently to produce fine specimens for winter use.

Saxifraga sarmentosa.   Aaron's Beard.   This well-known
plant is very useful for baskets, vases, and window-boxes.   The
leaves are roundish, dark green above, red below.   A variety
with variegated leaves is very pretty.   The plant forms long
runners on which young plants are produced.   Flowers whitish,
in loose panicles.   Rich, sandy, vegetable soil.

Sparmannia africana.   A tall and graceful shrub with
white flowers and large, palmate leaves.   For culture see
Hibiscus.

Stevia and **Eupatorium** are two allied plants of the Composite family.   They produce numerous very small white
flowers in winter.   Propagation and culture same as Chrysan-
themum.

Streptocarpus polyanthus is a very pretty plant of the
Gesnera family, producing large panicles of fine blue flowers on
erect peduncles.   The flowers are produced from the base of
large, single, stalkless leaves lying flat on the ground.   Requires no rest, can otherwise be grown in the same way as
other Gesneraceæ, which see.

Veronicas of the shrubby kind are very useful for window-
boxes, and also as common window-plants.   Propagation easy
by means of half-ripe cuttings.   Soil and treatment same as for
Jacobinia, but must be potted more firmly.   The flowers of
these handsome plants are either white or blue, in long axillary
spikes or racemes.

Viburnum Tinus is a fine evergreen shrub which flowers

early in spring if protected from frost. Large specimens in tubs are very fine for house decoration. The flowers are white, produced in umbels.

Vinca rosea. Crimson Periwinkle. This is an exceedingly fine and floriferous, erect-growing species. The flowers are large, white, pink, or crimson. Very easy to propagate by seeds, cuttings, or division. Light fibrous soil, full exposure to the sun, and liberal watering.

XIV

MISCELLANEOUS FOLIAGE-PLANTS

calypha is a robust plant of the Spurge family, with large cordate, exquisitely mottled leaves the ground-color of which is bronzy-green. They are easily grown plants, largely used for summer bedding in gardens, but also valuable as house plants. Propagation by soft-wooded cuttings or division; they thrive in any ordinary light and rich soil. Acalypha macrophylla has brown leaves with greenish spots; A. tricolor has bronzy leaves mottled and marbled with white and crimson.

Aloysia, or Lemon-scented Verbena, is a common enough plant with no ornamental value, but cultivated for the sake of its sweet-scented leaves. Grow from cuttings in ordinary soil.

Amaranthus tricolor. Three-colored Amaranth, with finely variegated leaves, green, yellow, and crimson, is a plant of dwarf habit and easy of culture. Propagated by soft-wooded cuttings, and will thrive in ordinary light soil.

Anthericum variegatum is a plant of the Lily family, with tufted variegated leaves, very useful for vases and window-boxes. Propagated by division, and will grow in any light, fibrous soil.

Aralia Sieboldii. One of the best foliage-plants for a

dwelling-house. It has large palmately lobed leaves and neat, compact habit. This useful plant can be raised from seeds which grow freely in a warm and shady position. The young seedlings should be repotted several times during the first summer. Plenty of air and a cool, half-shady position are best suitable in summer.

Araucaria excelsa. The Norfolk Pine is an elegant and robust-growing Conifer with regular feathery branches. Plants must be bought ; propagation not practicable in a house. It will thrive in rich fibrous soil. Handsome both as small plants and large specimens.

Aspidistra lurida fol. variegata.

Aspidistra, with green or variegated leaves, is the best foliage-plant for all purposes. Leaves broad, lanceolate on slender leaf, stalks growing from a thick and fleshy rootstock. This plant loves rich soil and plenty of water, and will do better in deep shade than most other plants. Easily propagated by division.

Aucuba japonica, an evergreen, almost hardy shrub with yellow-mottled leaves, grows to a large size and is useful for the porch or lawn in summer. Can be wintered in a light cellar. Any good, ordinary soil.

Bambusa nana. This is a graceful plant with lanceolate, grass-like leaves and slender, arching stems. Propagated by division. Soil rich and light. Abundant watering and partial shade.

Begonia Rex and some other species are exclusively grown for the sake of their beautiful leaves. They may be increased by means of leaf-cuttings inserted in sand, or by means of old, ripe leaves laid flat on the surface of sand, in a warm glass case, and cut across the principal veins. If kept moderately moist and warm, young plants will soon appear wherever the veins have been cut. These can be transplanted in the usual way in small pots in sandy, vegetable soil. Rex Begonias require a rather warm, shady position, a slight rest in winter, and liberal watering during the growing season. There are numerous varieties with mostly green, velvety leaves, marked and colored in various ways.

Bertolonia is a small genus of exquisitely colored foliage-plants, which are excellent for terrariums. They are dwarf in habit and form masses of leaves close to the ground. B. Van Houttii has hairy, ovate leaves finely spotted with pink and with broad magenta veins. B. marmorata, with silvery and deep bronzy-green leaves, is another fine species. The stems of both are short and succulent. Soil of equal parts loam, peat, leaf-mould and sand with broken pieces of charcoal.

Calatheas and **Marantas** are very fine, though rather tender, tropical plants, growing in deep shade among decaying leaves and vegetable matter. Most of them require excessive atmospheric moisture, and are therefore unfit for cultivation in a house except in double windows. The majority are dwarf plants with large spreading, variously colored leaves. All are adapted for growing in terrariums. They are very attractive when grown in suitable soil among miniature sandstone rocks. Increased by cuttings or division, and grow well in the same soil as Bertolonia. C. Mackoyana, leaves oblong, green, blotched along the midrib with white and yellow. C. Massangeana, leaves olive-green, velvety, middle portion silvery-gray with darker blotches. C. roseo-picta, leaves deep-green with a bright narrow rose-colored band on each side. C. roseo-line-ata, rather tall with leaves obliquely lined with rosy-red and white. M. concinna, leaves small, bright green, regularly marked with blotches of a deeper green. M. striata, dwarf species with green leaves closely striped with white and yellow.

Maranta roseo-lineata.

Croton or **Codiæum.** These are remarkable for their large, leathery, finely colored leaves, vying in brilliancy of color with the foliage of Caladium. Tall and woody plants requiring great heat and sunshine to develop their full beauty; they are admirably adapted for growing in dwelling-houses in this country. As small plants they are useful for table decoration, and when fine, large specimens, cannot be excelled as ornamental plants on the lawn in summer. Propagated by half-ripe cuttings in a warm place. When potting, a rich fibrous soil should be used and careful drainage is necessary. The plants should be grown in a sunny window, and must be liberally watered.   Frequent spraying of the foliage and washing to keep the leaves healthy and free from dust, will help to bring out the full beauty of these plants.

The finest varieties are: C. Andreanum, leaves large, broadly lanceolate with yellow veins; C. Disraeli, leaves hastate with red and golden veins; J. R. Rothschield, very broad, ovate, lanceolate leaves, bright green with crimson and yellow veins; C. undulatum, lanceolate leaves with wavy edges, bronze with red and crimson; C. pictum, somewhat similar to the last, with smooth edges; C. variegatum, heavily blotched leaves, green and yellow, with pale rose-colored leaf-stalks; C. elegans punctatum, leaves small, almost linear, green, spotted with bright yellow.   The varieties are very numerous, but the above are among the finest and most easily obtained kinds.

Coleus are common, soft-wooded bedding-plants with richly colored foliage, varying from pale yellow to deep purple and carmine, either one- or many-colored.   They are easy of culture and may be propagated by cuttings at any time of the year, and should be grown in rich fibrous soil.   Useful as specimen plants for the house or for planting in window-boxes and vases.

Coprosma Baueriana is the name of a handsome evergreen shrub with small ovate leaves, which are finely variegated with pure white.   It is almost hardy, and may be kept in a cool room during winter.   Propagated by soft-wooded cuttings in sand.   Pot, when rooted, in rich loamy soil, and pinch the young shoots slightly to form bushy specimens as the plants grow on.

Eranthemum.   Plants with yellow, variegated, blackish-purple or in various ways colored foliage, with succulent stems, and of a dwarf, bushy habit. The following varieties are extremely fine, and as easy of culture as Coleus :

E. albo - marginatum, large ovate leaves margined with white ; E. atropurpureum, leaves black-purple ; E. eldorado, bright yellow ; E. reticulatum, leaves broadly lanceolate, green, with numerous golden veins. The Eranthemums are suitable for all purposes, and are very ornamental when grown into good specimens.

Eucalyptus globulus. The blue gum-tree of Australia is a very rapid growing tree, and beautiful when young. Young plants are best, and should be raised every year from seed. Seed sown in sandy soil and kept in a moderately warm and shady place germinates readily. The seedlings should be potted singly in two- or three-inch pots in rich fibrous soil.

Farfugium grande is a strong-growing herbaceous plant, with large orbicular yellow-spotted leaves on tall leaf-stalks. Will grow rapidly in rich soil, and form fine specimen plants. Culture as simple and easy as that of Aspidistra, which see.

Ficus, or Rubber-plants, are common and popular everywhere. They should be grown in rich soil, and require liberal watering in summer. Besides the common Rubber-plant there are several other species of great beauty. The best are F. Cooperii, with large ovate-acuminate leaves with red midribs. F. Parcellii with tender green leaves, heavily blotched and marbled with white. These are especially valuable for the Southern States, and are easily propagated by means of cuttings in a warm place. F. elastica is more difficult to increase ; tops of old, straggling plants may be rooted in the following manner : Select ripe branches with several good leaves, and remove a ring of bark just below the lowest one. Split a small flower-pot lengthways and place the same round the branch, fill with moss or soil, and keep moist until thoroughly rooted, when the tops may be removed and potted without danger. The leaves should be frequently washed, and occasional spray-

Rubber-tree. *Ficus elastica.*

ings are to be recommended. Liberal top-dressings with safe artificial manures should be given to older plants.

Fittonias are fine trailing plants with large elliptical leaves. F. argyroneura has deep-green leaves with numerous pure white veins. F. Pearsii and F. gigantea have fine red-veined leaves. Cuttings root with the greatest of ease. Same soil and treatment as recommended for Bertolonia, and useful for the same purpose.

Grevillea robusta. Silk Oak. Leaves large, bipinnate, finely cut. Stem slender, erect. This is a very fine foliage-plant for the parlor, and when small one of the best plants for table decoration. Propagated by seed and cultivated like Aralia.

Iresine. A plant of the Amaranth family, with variegated or red foliage, mostly used for window-boxes and vases. The variety I. aureo-reticulata has green leaves with red veins and leaf-stalks, reticulated with yellow. I. Lindenii has red leaves and is a very common plant, grown along with Coleus under precisely the same treatment.

Isolepis is a small grass-like plant, of a tufty habit, with thread-like pendulous leaves. It is very useful in small pots

for edgings to flower-stands, vases, and boxes. This plant
should be kept in a small state by frequent division. Rich,
but sandy, vegetable soil suits it best.

Kæmpferias are interesting herbaceous plants with fleshy
root-stock and roots, and flower early in spring before the
leaves appear. The flowers are very delicate and beautiful, and
very sweet-scented. The plants are, however, chiefly grown
as foliage-plants. The best one for this purpose is the variety
named Gilbertii, with broad and long Dracena-like leaves in
dense tufts. Foliage variegated with white. The Kæmpferias should be allowed to rest during the earlier part of winter,

after which the roots should be
cleaned, potted in very fibrous
and light soil, and started in a
warm room. The flowers will
soon appear and remain for a
considerable period, after which
the leaves develop.

Ficus Parcelli.

Laurus nobilis. The Sweet
Bay is an evergreen tree with
lanceolate, leathery leaves. Cultivated in different ways, with a
stem and globular crowns, or as
bushy or pyramidal plants with
leaves down to the ground. Rich
fibrous loam is the best soil. The
plants may be kept in a cool
and light cellar in winter, to be used in summer for lawn
decoration.

Mimosa pudica. Sensitive plant. This is a very interesting as well as beautiful plant, with doubly pinnate leaves, sen-

sitive to the touch.   Plants can be raised early in spring from seeds, with the greatest of ease.   They will do well in any oi dinary soil.

The seeds can be sown, two or three in a small pot.   After germination the strongest should be kept.   Plenty of water and good drainage are essential.

Panicum variegatum, a grass with white-variegated foliage, of a creeping habit, is very useful for edging window-boxes and vases, or in pots for flower-stands.   Propagated by cuttings of trailing shoots.   Grows well in sandy, fibrous soil in a half-shady position.

Pelargonium crispum, with roundish leaves. *P. fragrans* with trilobate, and *P. quercifolium* with deeply incised leaves remotely resembling oak-leaves, are grown for the sake of their strongly scented foliage, under their respective names of Apple-, Nutmeg-, and Rose-geraniums.   Propagated and grown as Geraniums.

Pellionia pulchra.   A neat and beautiful foliage-plant with fleshy, trailing stems and obliquely cordate, leathery leaves of a blackish-green color, dull purple beneath.   Will grow easily from cuttings in any ordinary soil.   Handsome for terrariums.

Peperomia is a small genus of very dwarf foliage-plants of neat habit, very useful for edging or for growing in terrariums.   P. argyrea, leaves orbicular, green, marbled with white. P. Saundersii, leaves orbicular, succulent, green banded with white.   Easily increased by division and grow well in light, sandy, vegetable soil.

Pilea muscosa.   Artillery-plant.   Soft-wooded, erect plants with very small, reddish leaves, and minute flowers that open suddenly when breathed upon, dispersing the fine white pollen. Propagated by cuttings and grown in light, fibrous soil.

Ruellia Devosiana. A beautiful and compact plant, with ,all lanceolate leaves, velvety green with white pencillings ,ove, purple beneath. Flowers unimportant. Will grow well in rich vegetable soil, in a moist and warm place such as a terrarium. Easy to increase by means of cuttings.

Sanchesia nobilis, a plant of the Acanthus family, with short stems and large oblong-acuminate leaves marked with yellow bands along the veins. Propagated by cuttings which root readily in a warm place. Soil rich and fibrous, abundant watering in summer and a half-shady position.

Sanchesia nobilis.

Sonerila Margaritacea. A fine foliage-plant with ovate lanceolate leaves of a dark glossy green, with white spots in longitudinal rows on the upper surface. Flowers pretty, rose-purple in small corymbs. This is a fine plant for the terrarium, where it should be grown in a well-drained position in sandy, vegetable soil.

Stenandrium Lindenii. This is a very effective foliage-plant, nearly related to the Eranthemums. The leaves are obovate in outline, tapering toward the base. The color is of a rich, velvety green with yellow variegations along the veins. This is a fine plant for terrariums or for any warm room. It requires shade and moisture, and prefers rich vegetable soil with plenty of sand. The procumbent branches will root easily, and when separated soon form nice plants.

Strobilanthus is a new kind of bedding-plant, with leaves richly suffused with steel-blue and purple. Will probably prove useful in vases and window-boxes. Can be grown as Coleus.

Umbrella plant. Cyperus alternifolius, with green leaves, and Cyperus laxus, with variegated ones ; both are sold under the above name. They are very neat and useful plants when well grown, requiring plenty of moisture, good drainage, and rich fibrous soil. Progagated by cuttings of the tall " leaves " or by division.

XV

CLIMBING AND TRAILING PLANTS

VINES and creepers in great variety may be grown to perfection in any house. Their graceful habits render them especially useful for home decoration. Some may be trained around the windows and doors to make rich and beautiful festoons of leaves and flowers. Many, as the common Ivy, will grow in deep shade and require little or no care, others enjoy light and sunshine, but are also easy of culture. Boxes with neat trelliswork may be employed to form beautiful living screens of climbing plants and vines. In selecting this class of plants for the house, care should be taken to choose varieties that will develop their full beauty in a comparatively short time, as many otherwise valuable kinds flower only when large and old, and such varieties are always disappointing. The following kinds, when grown for the sake of their flowers, are free-flowering and easy of culture. Some are foliage-plants, and should always be ornamental.

Allamanda. This is an elegant, straggling shrub with long and slender branches, producing large trumpet-shaped flowers of a deep yellow color, and rather long lanceolate leaves in whorls. Propagated by half-ripe cuttings, and will do well in a rich, fibrous soil. When the summer growth is finished late in fall the plants should have a thorough rest in winter, but must not be allowed to lose the leaves. The ripened branches of the previous year will produce clusters of flowers in spring. The young shoots, after flowering, should be pruned back, and watering should be gradually increased as the young growth develops. These plants enjoy plenty of heat and sunshine. The best varieties are: A. Hendersonii, A. Schottii, and A. nerifolia.

Thunbergia.

Aristolochia. Of these curious plants, the Dutchman's Pipes or Birthworts, there are several small and elegant forms producing large flowers of grotesque shape. The variety, elegans, is the best for common use. Other very interesting kinds are: A. grandiflora and A. ridicula. Soil of equal parts loam, leaf-mould, well-rotted manure, and sand is very suitable. Propagated by cuttings. A warm and sunny position and plenty of water during the growing season are necessary.

Asparagus plumosus and its variety, nanus, are, the first a fine climber, and the second a neat fern-like plant with feathery foliage. Both may be increased by division or seed. The dwarf variety is very useful for table decoration. They will thrive in the same kind of soil as Aristolochia.

Bignonia capensis is a handsome creeper with pinnate leaves and large trusses of orange-scarlet flowers early in spring. It can be kept low and bushy by means of pruning. Should be grown in a sunny position, in rich, fibrous soil, and requires plenty of water while growing.

Bougainvillea glabra is a large-growing, woody plant, producing numerous flowers which are surrounded by purple bracts, making the plant very showy when in bloom. It is easily grown in a house, in the same soil as Allamanda and with the same treatment. There is a dwarf, bushy variety called Sanderiana.

Cissus discolor, a beautiful vine with cordate, velvety green leaves mottled with white and pink on the upper surface ; red below. Useful for vases and brackets ; will grow best in a terrarium or double window. Propagated by cuttings. Soil as for Aristolochia.

Clematis indivisa lobata. Fine climber, with leathery, ternate leaves and a profusion of white, daisy-like flowers in large panicles early in summer. Very useful and exceedingly beautiful for a sunny window.

Clerodendron Balfourii. This plant flowers when quite small, producing immense clusters of crimson flowers with large white calyx. The foliage is fine, of a deep-green color. This is one of the best climbers for window culture. Soil rich and fibrous. Propagation by cuttings.

Cobæa is a very rapid-growing climber, with large bell-shaped flowers of a greenish-purple color and pinnate tendriled leaves. Propagated by seed and treated as an annual. Useful outside of windows or for the veranda.

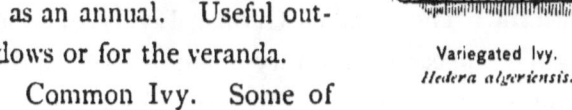

Variegated Ivy.
Hedera algeriensis.

Hedera. Common Ivy. Some of the finer varieties, especially the variegated ones, are beautiful for all purposes. They will grow in deep shade, and require little or no attention except an occasional watering. Some of the varieties are finely mottled and marbled with white or yellow, others have the foliage broadly margined with white. They also differ in the size and shape of their leaves. The best varieties are : algeriensis, marginata, and marmorata. The common green Irish Ivy is also beautiful.

Hoya carnosa. Wax-flower. So called because of the waxy appearance of the small clustered flowers. The leaves are thick and fleshy, either green or variegated. Propagated by cuttings. For potting use fibrous soil and good drainage.

Jasminum. The Jessamines are pretty climbing plants, with white or yellow fragrant flowers. All are easy of culture, and very ornamental when in flower. The variety known as J. gracillimum is the best for general use. Propagated by cuttings. Soil as for Aristolochia.

Kennedya Maryattæ. A fine, slender climber of the Pea-family, with large scarlet flowers in axillary clusters. Leaves trifoliate, hairy, with wavy edges. Rapid - growing and one of the finest climbers known. Propagated by seeds. Soil as above.

Manettia is a neat little climber, with small, broadly lanceo-lated leaves and tubular flowers of a bright-scarlet color with yellow segments. Easily increased by cuttings. Soil as above.

Maurandia. A class of plants with pretty blue or purple flowers. Tender climbers propagated by seeds, and treated as Cobæa.

Mikania. The so-called German Ivy. An American plant of Ivy-like appearance, a very rapid grower, and one of the best climbers for a house. Propagated by means of cuttings.

Passiflora. Passion-flowers are well-known plants with large, beautiful flowers, white, blue, or scarlet, generally very showy and of peculiar structure. The variety known as Elliot's white, P. cœrulea alba, is a pure white form of the old blue Passion flower, and deserves a place in every home. The scarlet flowering varieties are less common, but comparatively easy to obtain. Propagated by cuttings and grown in rich soil.

Solanum jasminoides is a very fine climber of the Potato family, producing large clusters of pure white flowers. This is useful for vases, baskets, and window-boxes, and is perhaps the best plant of its class for either purpose. Propagated by cuttings. Will do well in rich fibrous soil.

Stigmaphyllum ciliatum. Butterfly Vine. One of the prettiest and most floriferous climbers for a warm, sunny position. The flowers are bright yellow, the leaves heart-shaped. This beautiful plant will do well in very small pots, is always clean and free from insects. The slender stems and its graceful habit make it one of the most ornamental plants.

White Passion Flower.
Passiflora carulea alba.

Thunbergia alata. Tender annual with white or buff-colored flowers, easily propagated by seeds and treated as Cobæa.

Th. erecta is a woody plant, with dark willow-like leaves, and large axillary flowers of a fine blue color. Propagated by cuttings. This is a fine, bushy plant.

Smilax is a well-known green-house climber, extensively grown in this country for florist work. It does not, as a rule, thrive in a house.

Zeneria scabra. A plant of the Gourd-family, with palmate

leaves and a profusion of white flowers, followed by very ornamental scarlet berries, is a very rapid-growing vine easily propagated by seeds.

There are a number of trailing and creeping plants generally
grown in baskets and vases, or in window-boxes and pots.
They are of graceful habit and very ornamental when well
grown.   Among these are :

Campanula garganica, a bell-flower with slender, trailing
stems and numerous blue flowers during spring and summer.   Very ornamental.

Ficus repens.   This is a very small and slender vine with
creeping stems and air-roots, attaching itself to a wall or other
object, to which it grows closely, forming a fine mass of deep-
green leaves.   Useful for vases and hanging baskets.

Glechoma hederacea, with variegated leaves, is a form of a
common weed that has lately become important as an ornamental plant.   It is very pretty for hanging baskets and window-boxes.   The leaves are orbicular green with white margin.

Pelargonium peltatum.   The Ivy-leaved Geranium is an
exceptionally pretty plant, with numerous single or double
flowers of various colors, in large clusters.   For culture see
Geranium.

Torenia.   Nice little plants with snap-dragon-like flowers,
either blue or white.   Raised from seeds in spring.

Tradescantia.   Wandering Jew.   Three or four varieties
with green, white-striped ; or red, white, and green foliage.
Stem and leaves succulent.   Pretty for hanging baskets.

Verbenas are also useful for indoor use as well as for window-boxes and vases.   They are well known and need no description.   Should be raised by means of seed or cuttings early
in spring.

Vinca major with white or yellow variegated foliage; has long slender, hanging stems, and is one of the most ornamental plants for vases and window-boxes.

All the above are easily increased by cuttings, and require no special treatment.

The little blue **Lobelia** so commonly seen in gardens, is also useful for all purposes. So are various kinds of **Indian Cress** (**Tropæolum**), all easily raised from seed. There is a variegated Tropæolum commonly grown in green-houses, propagated by cuttings.

PLANTS WITH ORNAMENTAL FRUIT

THE plants producing ornamental fruit in a house are few in number and not important. The following are very ornamental :

Ardisia crenulata. Shrub, with dark green foliage, clusters of white flowers, dotted red followed by clusters of scarlet berries. Propagated by cuttings and grown in rich, fibrous soil in a cool and airy apartment. Height two or three feet.

Nertera depressa is a dwarf, tender plant finely tufted, with slender trailing stems, and numerous small red berries on the surface. This is an easily grown plant suitable for terrariums or Wardian cases. Seeds or cuttings.

Rivina humilis. Rapid-growing plant of the Poke-berry-family, of an erect habit, with long racemes of scarlet berries. Grows very easily from seeds, and needs no special culture.

Solanum capsicastrum is a compact shrub of the Potato family, producing numerous berries of a deep scarlet color. Ornamental for table decoration, and easily grown from seeds or cuttings. Pinch the young plants to produce bushy specimens. Water carefully when the fruit is being formed, and sparingly when ripe. The fruit ripens in November or December and remains on the plants for several months.

BULBS AND HARDY PLANTS FOR FORCING

ilium lancifolium is one of the finest flowering bulbs for forcing. The flowers are large, with narrow recurved petals of a rosy-red color dotted with darker spots. It flowers late in spring and summer when forced, or late in fall when left in the open ground. L. Harrisii, the white trumpet-like flowers of which are universally used by florists, flowers early in the season and is generally at its best about Easter. L. candidum, the white lily, is well known, and is quite as beautiful in pots as in the garden border.

Lance-leaved Lily.
Lilium lancifolium.

Freesia. This is a dwarf lily-like plant with white trumpet-like flowers in large clusters. It flowers early in spring or summer. The bulbs are small, and several should be put together in a four- or five-inch pot.

Crocus, Tulips, and **Hyacinths** are very beautiful when forced for early winter-flowering. They can all be had in flower about Christmas-time.   Hyacinths can be grown either in ordinary pots or in water, in glasses made for the purpose. Crocus and Tulips should be put several together in small pots.   They are very showy when in flower, and the bulbs are very cheap.   The single varieties of both Hyacinths or Tulips are the best for every purpose.

Narcissi of all kinds, including the Chinese Sacred Lily and the fragrant Poets' Narcissus, are very useful for winter-flowering.   The little white Galanthus also looks well in pots or massed in small shallow pans.   The Chinese Lily is frequently grown in pretty glass bowls filled with clean pebbles and water.

The soil used for all bulbs should be composed of equal parts of loam, well-rotted manure, or leaf-mould and sand, and the pots must be well drained.

After potting a good watering is necessary.   They are then placed in a cool, dark cellar until rooted, when they can be brought into a warm apartment one by one, as required to keep up a continuous supply of flowering plants.   Bulbs should not be buried too deep in the soil.

Among other hardy plants useful for forcing the **Anemones** take a prominent place.   The scarlet anemone is the most showy one and the best.

The **Japanese Spirea** (Hoteja japonica) when forced is exceptionally beautiful.   The white flowers are produced in very large panicles, and the bright-green compound leaves spreading below make a beautiful contrast.   This is one of the most useful plants for forcing, and may be had in flower for a considerable period.

Many **Stone-crops** (Saxifraga), **Primroses,** and other herbaceous plants are very good for forcing.   The **Christmas Rose**

(Helleborus niger) has large pure white flowers, and may be had in full bloom at Christmas.

Several shrubby plants as **Azaleas** and **Mountain Laurels,** when well established in pots and brought into warm rooms. will flower early and make a good effect. Hardy ferns and some of the choice wild flowers can be forced in the same way as bulbs.

The **Violet** is perhaps the most popular of all plants for this purpose. Planted in masses in shallow pans or neat wooden boxes of a convenient size, in about two or three inches of rich fibrous soil, it will grow and flower profusely. Plant single crowns about three inches apart in the box or pan. Water thoroughly and grow in a cool cellar close to a north window, where the plants can remain cool and partially shaded through summer. All runners should be removed, as the original crowns will be sufficient to fill the space. In fall the plants must be cleaned, all dead or withered leaves should be removed. The surface of the soil should afterward be mulched with chopped moss or covered with fine pebbles. During winter, when the plants are desired to bloom, a warm, sunny position is the best. As the pans and boxes become covered with flowers, they may be brought into the sitting-room or parlor. Moderate watering is to be recommended at all times.

INDEX

www.ingramcontent.com/pod-product-compliance
Lightning Source LLC
Chambersburg PA
CBHW020229030726
47497CB00009B/3013